How to Transform Your Life With IMPACT: Unlock the Best of You

How to Transform Your Life With IMPACT: Unlock the Best of You
ISBN: 978-1-8384749-0-4

First published in Great Britain
in 2021 through Amazon self-publishing
service Kindle Direct Publishing.

Produced in the UK by The Book Writers' Resource
www.thebookwritersresource.co.uk

Disclaimer:

Contents

HOW TO
TRANSFORM YOUR LIFE WITH
IMPACT
UNLOCK THE BEST OF YOU

Mark Evans

Introduction

When someone meets me for the first time as a coach and therapist, I want them to feel straightaway that I am the right person for them. To achieve this I need to demonstrate that I can help them to successfully overcome their difficulties and achieve their challenges. My aim is for this book to have the same IMPACT on you. I want the title 'How To Transform Your Life With IMPACT' to come true for you.

The subject of this book, The IMPACT Model, has been tried and tested over thousands of hours of practice and with thousands of clients. From 18-year-old university students, to middle-aged business people, to people in retirement, I have seen people use The IMPACT Model to transform their lives.

Whatever prompted you to buy this book, be it a crisis, a sense of 'stuckness' or simply a desire to be more and do more in life, the six stages of The IMPACT Model contain the knowledge and ideas, the techniques and strategies, to make the difference you are after.

The IMPACT Model

The six stages of The IMPACT Model are:

I – a conversation with IMPACT. All of us have experienced feelings of hope and relief when we talk to someone who knows exactly what to say to us. And all of us have felt frustration and disappointment when a conversation fails to give us what we need. Persistent difficulties and insurmountable challenges mean that our existing conversations are missing important qualities and characteristics. A Conversation with Impact contains what we need to make the difference we are after.

M – Meaning. Making progress often depends on us making sense of why things are as they are. Without a clear understanding we remain a mystery to ourselves, making progress difficult or even impossible.

P – Patterns. Positive change is dependent on us understanding what we do a lot of that is not working, and what we are not doing enough of that is. Unless and until we are able to step back from and understand our problematic patterns we will struggle to move forwards in life.

A – Acceptance. Achieving personal growth can stretch, challenge and reward us. However, if our goals and expectations are unrealistic, we can become demoralised and exhausted. When this happens our Fantasy-Reality Gap has become too large and the only way to close it is through acceptance.

C – Challenge. If we had the solution we would already be the person we want to be, and we would already be living the life we want to lead. The challenge is to find out what stands in our way and the strategies to get around it.

T – Transformation. We all want to reach our final destination when our challenges and difficulties have been dealt with and overcome. And yet if it were that easy, we would all be there by now. Only an effective approach to transformation will get us to our final destination.

Why have I written this book?

The short answer to this question is this book is a way I can make a positive difference to your life. Conversations change lives and this book is my conversation with you to change yours. A great deal has been written on the two main areas of my work—coaching and therapy. The reason for this large body of knowledge is due in part to the ongoing contribution of practitioners like myself and the people we work with. New approaches to age-old human problems are like new maps to the same 'territory.' Yes, countless people have visited the 'territory' you are on now, but that territory is constantly evolving, requiring new maps. I do believe wholeheartedly that my contribution is one that can add to, rather than simply duplicate what is already out there. If I did not, I would not have written The IMPACT Model. And everyone has a book in them apparently.

Who is this book for?

The list below is not a randomised item assortment, but very real cases that have been brought to my attention from clients. It is not an exhaustive list, as humans are complex creatures with a myriad of personal concerns which can be developed.

This book can be used for:

- an enforced change such as redundancy or illness.
- a chosen life change.
- multiple or single concerns.
- a crisis.
- to unlock as yet untapped potential.
- to improve what works well.

- highlighting past, present or future concerns.
- personal and/or Professional Development.
- identity.
- career change.
- mental health.
- wellbeing.
- relationships.
- bereavement.
- loneliness.
- confidence building.
- developing new skills and abilities.
- therapeutic guidance.

What is this book for?

"Hi Mark – It's been a while, which I suppose is a good thing. Just thought I would get in touch to say thanks for all your help. It has completely changed me as a person and completely changed the course of my life. I'm now working in youth and community work and enjoying every minute. So out of my comfort zone working with teenagers, but it's great. Anyway, not going to bore you with all the details, but just to say thanks for everything you have done for me." Laura

Laura's story will feature in full at the end of this Introduction. Her story is a remarkable one that culminated for me at least, in the above message. I was privileged to have worked with Laura for around a year. Her transformation is a testament to what people are capable of given the right support.

I want the IMPACT Model to be for you what it was for Laura. Firstly, as a manual and a guide to take you from where you are now in life to where you want to be. Regardless of your start or desired end point the IMPACT model will work for you because its six stages cover the spectrum of change and transformation that is possible. Secondly, as a map to help you locate where you are in your own journey of transformation. It will show you where you are now and how you got there, and it will show you where you are now and the distance left to your destination. Finally, I see the IMPACT model as a diagnostic tool. Whenever you are stuck or making progress, you will be able to understand why through reference to any of the six stages.

How does this book work?

"I want you to leave with more than you came in with."

I say this to my clients at the start of their coaching or therapy and every appointment afterwards. If someone leaves an appointment with what they came in with, then what was the point of seeing me? A client has to leave thinking that meeting me was worthwhile. The same goes for this book. Each page and section have been written to give you something you didn't know or have before that connects to the difficulties and challenges you face. My aim is for this book to make the difference you are after by giving you what you need to overcome your difficulties and achieve your challenges. If I succeed maybe you will let me know?

My personal and professional experience reinforces my belief that the model's six stages are non-negotiable for successful change and transformation. As the author I would love for you to read it through once and having gained an appreciation for the model, to read it a second time and apply the model to your own situation. This might be wishful thinking on my part, so I have endeavoured to write it so that you can get to work straightaway. Each chapter makes sense in relation to the next, as do the many activities for self-discovery, learning and reflection. Where you are in your own journey of change and transformation will, I imagine, determine which stages you connect with the most at any one time and how long you spend on them.

A question I am often asked by clients is how long coaching or therapy takes. In my early career I tried to be helpful by being specific. Now I don't get into the 'prediction' game because I proved to be a poor clairvoyant. The same applies to this book. How long will it take? How long should you spend on each Chapter or activity? My answer is I can't say. I want my clients to value themselves and commit to doing what is necessary. If I do my job effectively then in my experience people do. The same applies to you as a reader of this book. If it is well written, then I think you will commit too.

How will you get past a stage if you get stuck? Or how will you get past a difficulty or challenge you have been stuck on? As a practitioner I assume that my clients will get stuck and/or we will get stuck together at some stage. My response is always to persevere and trust that a way through will be found. As a coach and therapist I trust that my knowledge and experience, plus my belief in my clients' potential will produce positive outcomes for them. The same applies to this book. I trust that it contains what you need, and I believe in your potential to make this book work for you. So, if you get stuck reading this book, be kind to and patient with yourself. Go back to the Chapters and activities and like a great story trust they will give you something new each time.

Activities, tasks and exercises

In addition to the many activities, tasks and exercises included in each chapter, are standalone examples situated in between chapters. I hope you will get just as much value from these.

Doing it yourself and doing it with others

This book is for you individually, but there is much that assumes the direct or indirect involvement of at least one other person, as someone else is bound to play a part at some point in your transformation.

This is why the first stage of the IMPACT model is especially important because it addresses your existing conversations and whether they are making the difference you are after. If they aren't, then my IMPACT questionnaires will show you what qualities and characteristics are missing from those conversations. This information is gold dust because when you do find the right person to talk to, it can be shared with them.

Inspiration

Since 2005 when I first qualified as a therapist, I have worked with some truly amazing and inspirational people. Their stories and experiences will crop up throughout the book hopefully as a source of inspiration for you, too. All identifying details have been changed significantly to ensure privacy and confidentiality is maintained.

Laura's story

"In the two years or so prior to seeing Mark, I had surgery for cancer and developed an intestinal condition. Before that and for more years than I care to remember, I was suffering from what I now know to be Post-Traumatic Stress Disorder as the result of two traumatic incidents. My professional life, while successful, was ruining my health. I had avoided therapy because I saw it as a failure, but despite my best efforts my antidepressants weren't helping. I was suicidal and if I'm being honest, it was only the thought of my husband and children that stopped me from going through with it. My health became so poor that my GP reluctantly had to take my driving licence away from me. Looking back, losing my ability to drive was the worst thing of all. Gone was my independence.

I is for IMPACT

My GP asked me to reconsider therapy, so I went on a counselling directory and saw Mark's photo and profile. In our first session he asked me why I had chosen him. I told him that in his photo he looked kind. I understood the meaning behind the name of his business, so in addition to kindness I told him I also needed him to accept me, to not judge me, regardless of what I came through his door with each week. Although it took me several months to finally talk about some stuff, I knew that I had to if I was to get better.

M is for MEANING

I'd always seen myself as a miscalculation on my parents' part, an error. My parents were very young when I was born, and this was the conclusion I came to. Mark made a connection between my poor mental health and the dim view I had of myself. The knowledge he shared with me about identity and emotions was a genuine missing piece of the jigsaw. Mark talked a lot about my negative self. He suggested that this was who I thought I was and that our job was to get me to see otherwise. I'll admit I found this confusing at first as, if this wasn't who I was, then who was I? As it turned out, I was the one who booked the first therapy session. Turkeys don't vote for Christmas—Mark said—and negative selves don't book therapy sessions. Understanding that my negative self would not have accessed therapy because therapy is a threat to their dominance, put me in contact with the parts of myself which I now realise were responsible for my recovery.

P is for PATTERNS

Therapy helped me to identify one particularly destructive pattern. I did not consider myself as important and was unable to do positive things for myself. For example, I often left work very late— sometimes in the small hours—and I would wait for a night bus to take me back home. Despite earning more than enough to pay for a taxi, I saw such expense as an indulgence. This pattern of self-neglect was also reflected in my prioritisation of others. Focusing on patterns helped me correct this pattern (and others) which was not helping me. I had habituated the pattern that I could only be a good person if I helped others. I was simply the person who everyone else went to because I never said "no" to a request for help. This pattern in my relationships was, I believe, killing me.

A is for ACCEPTANCE

Prior to therapy, I would never have considered myself a good person, someone with esteem and worth. In therapy I came to accept that I was not a mistake. Hearing Mark tell me, repeatedly, that I had worth as a human being eventually sank in. I either accepted what he said or had to accuse him of lying. I also came to accept that other people and life events had to share some responsibility for who I was and the life I had led. This had been pointed out to me before, but accepting it felt like an excuse. So I stopped rescuing and providing for everyone else. The fear that putting myself first sometimes would result in people abandoning me never materialised. There were some who didn't like being told, "no," and they disappeared from my life, but if that was a bad thing then why did I feel better? I still gave a lot of myself to my friends and family, but I got the balance right between them and me. I came to accept that fundamentally changing my approach to myself and my life was not a mark of failure, but one of achievement.

C is for CHALLENGE

While my overall health was improving, I knew I had to find alternative employment if I was to make a full recovery. This meant changing career. This was not a new realisation, but simply thinking about what this would involve caused me to have panic attacks. I came to see that it was not the goal of changing that was overwhelming, but my strategy to achieve it. Over time, I developed a realistic, achievable approach to changing my career that satisfied my need for progress without causing me to panic I would never find one. That was my worst fear, that I would never find one. Everything else depended on this outcome and I can't tell you the relief I felt when I knew it would be possible. Mark found a level of challenge that I could accept. Once I knew it was going to happen, I was able to start thinking about what I could do next. This was another challenge, but I had a large network of contacts that Mark suggested I tap into. One of those resulted in the role I am doing now.

T is for TRANSFORMATION

At the end of therapy I was fundamentally a different person leading a fundamentally different life. Virtually everything has changed: my career, the number of hours I work, my relationships and my health. Two great days were when my intestinal condition was brought under control and I got my driving licence back. I initially chose Mark because he looked kind, but his IMPACT model showed me where I had been going wrong and what I could do about it. I changed my career and I am now a mentor working with disadvantaged young adults. I walk my dogs and enjoy my holidays. And most importantly my family no longer have to worry about me being around." Laura

I is for IMPACT

To overcome our difficulties and challenges in life we need to have the right conversations with ourselves and others at the right time. When we don't, our difficulties and challenges can persist. All of us have experienced feelings of hope, relief and excitement when a conversation gives us exactly what we need; and all of us have felt despair, disappointment and frustration when a conversation fails to do so.

When someone talks to me in my professional capacity as a coach or therapist, my working assumption is that their existing conversations are not making the difference they are after. If they were, they would not be sat in front of me. And when someone buys a self-help book like this one, I come to a similar conclusion. This doesn't mean I assume everyone's conversations are unhelpful, it just means that for one reason or another they are not making the difference they are after.

When we want to transform ourselves and the lives we lead—we need a 'Conversation with IMPACT.'

BOX 1

A conversation can take different forms. It can be interpersonal i.e. involving someone else. It can be intrapersonal i.e. just with ourselves. And increasingly it can be with someone who sounds human, but that is 'artificial.'

A conversation can take place in a variety of contexts such as in our heads, at home or work. They can occur in the same physical space or virtually, using a variety of different technologies.

The types of conversations we have can overlap. Who hasn't engaged in a conversation with themselves while sat with others? Or chatted face-to-face while texting someone elsewhere? Or found themselves talking to a piece of technology as if they were a real person?

I like to think that I am having a conversation with you, the reader, through this book.

What defines a Conversation with Impact is not the type but the outcome, and that is what makes the difference you are after.

The first stage

The six stages of my IMPACT model are non-negotiable for successful change and transformation. What is also non-negotiable is the position of the I stage. On page 3 are the six stages of the IMPACT model and the outcomes achieved by completing them. Only a Conversation with Impact will get you through the other five stages because no other type of conversation can help you to:

- make the difference you are after - IMPACT
- make sense of why things are as they are – MEANING
- identify unhelpful, negative patterns and replace them with helpful, positive ones – PATTERNS
- find acceptance as your real self, someone with potential – ACCEPTANCE
- make challenge work for you, not against you - CHALLENGE
- learn the art of transformation - TRANSFORMATION.

If it were untrue that we needed a Conversation With Impact to achieve our transformation, then I would be doing something else right now. There would be no need for coaches, therapists and self-help books because you (and everyone else) would know how to get yourself through to Transformation and beyond.

In this chapter, I will help you to identify what is missing from your existing conversations so that you can begin to have Conversations with Impact. This voyage of discovery will involve both the conversations you have with yourself and with others. When it comes to yourself, we will look at how you can improve your self-talk or inner dialogue. And when it comes to other people, we will look at how your conversations with them can be improved and also whether you need somebody new to talk to.

What is a 'Conversation with Impact?'

A 'Conversation with Impact' is one that contains the qualities and characteristics that make the difference you are after.

By including previously missing qualities and characteristics, such as trust, positivity and helpful ideas, a Conversation with Impact demonstrates that it is different. And it is this difference that creates the IMPACT because it gives someone the experience of a conversation that can resolve the difficulties and challenges, they are facing. I never underestimate the impact this can have because of the hope, relief, and excitement it generates. When I do my job well and give someone such a conversation, I see them visibly change in front of me as reality hits them that I can and will help.

A Conversation with Impact always gives someone more than they started with and as a result they are changed by the experience. This is because a Conversation with Impact is based on an effective relationship that brings with it new ideas and perspectives, goals and strategies, knowledge and information.

A Conversation with Impact positively influences our other conversations because it removes the pressure from them to make the difference we are after. It changes how much we talk to ourselves and others; what we talk to ourselves and others about; and even whether certain conversations need to continue. Finding a Conversation with Impact means we no longer waste precious time and energy engaging in conversations that take us further away from where we want to be in life.

> "I would just batter myself with self-criticism. Give myself a daily diet of self-sabotage, 'that wasn't good enough,' or, 'really? That's it?' I now understand why I did this and how not to." Graham

The 'Conversations With Impact' questionnaires

On pages 5 and 6 are the two questionnaires I have designed to help you to identify what you need from a conversation to make the difference you are after. One questionnaire addresses the conversations you are having with yourself and the other relates to your conversations with others. Both include what I consider to be the essential qualities and characteristics of a Conversation with Impact. Completing them will enable you to build up a detailed picture of your existing conversations and what you can do to improve them.

Statement	Score	Statement	Score
I trust the person		They understand me and what I need from them	
I feel respected by them		They have the ideas, skills and knowledge I need	
They do not judge me and accept me for who I am			
The conversation follows my agenda not theirs		They believe in me and my potential for change	
They give me the time that i need		I feel challenged by them in a good way	
They respect my need for confidentiality		I feel they genuinely listen to me	
I can say what I really want to them		They are truly interested in me	
They help me to make sense of my situation		The help me set clear, realistic goals and strategies	
They help me find solutions		My conversations with them make a difference	
		They have the X-Factor	

Statement	Score	Statement	Score
I trust myself		I believe in myself and my potential for change	
I respect myself		I challenge myself in a good way	
I do not judge myself and accept me for who I am		I genuinely listen to myself	
My self-talk follows my agenda, not others'		I am truly interested in myself	
I give myself the time I need		I can make sense of my situation	
I respect my confidentiality and do not overshare		I set clear, realistic goals and strategies for myself	
I can say what I really want to myself		I can find solutions by myself	
I understand myself and what I need from me		My conversations and self-talk make a difference	
I have the ideas, skills and knowledge I need		I have the X-Factor	
I can look at myself objectively			

Current conversations

What conversations should you include? The list below gives some suggestions but include any that are relevant to the difficulties and challenges you are facing. In other words, if you enter into a daily discussion with the owner of your local corner shop, this might be one to leave out.

Conversations to consider are those had with:

- yourself
- partners

- family
- friends
- colleagues
- bosses
- professionals such as therapists, coaches or mentors
- social and cultural representatives such as teachers or community figures
- religious and spiritual leaders
- artificial interfaces such as apps and other technologies.

Both questionnaires work in exactly the same way. Start by listing the conversations you feel are relevant to your situation. Then for each conversation, choose a number between 1 and 7 that reflects the degree to which the conversation possesses each quality or characteristic listed in the questionnaires. When scoring your conversations, consider the importance of each quality or characteristic to you. If one is not important to you i.e. it makes no difference one way or the other, just give it a 7. For those that are important to you, score it appropriately. Remember to keep a copy of your individual conversations and their scores.

The number of completed questionnaires should equal the number of conversations you selected originally.

What did you discover?

It is important to remember there are no right or wrong combinations of qualities and characteristics, which means there are no right or wrong scores. However, in my experience:

- conversations with mostly low scores (3 or below)

      tend to make things worse

- conversations with mostly medium scores (4 or 5) tend to result in little or no change
- conversations with mostly high scores (6 or 7) tend to result in positive change.

Looking at your scores, what do they say about your current conversations and how they might explain the existence and persistence of your difficulties and challenges?

Conversations with yourself:

I urge you not to neglect the conversations with yourself.

These conversations will be the one constant as you commit to changing and transforming yourself. My aim is for these conversations to become JUST as important and effective to you as any other. I know from my own personal and professional experience that the conversations we have with ourselves play a pivotal role in our lives. When we don't have someone else to talk to, being able to give ourselves a Conversation with Impact is essential. And even when we have great support around us, it is rarely enough by itself.

> "I learnt what an effective conversation was and that those I was having with myself were very far from being effective. Now my conversations with myself are effective. I have become my own life coach." Katherine

Looking at the questionnaire for conversations with yourself and your scores for each quality and characteristic, ask yourself:

- what do you need to maintain?
- what do you need to find more of?
- what would make them a Conversation with Impact?

If you have given yourself only low or mostly low-to-medium scores i.e. your self-talk is negative, there are usually good reasons for this such as low self-esteem, poor mental health or toxic, unhealthy relationships. If this is what you have discovered, then the next five chapters will help you identify what you can do about your situation.

If you have given yourself mainly high scores, ask yourself if you are already giving yourself a Conversation with Impact. If you are then you will know because your difficulties and challenges are being overcome, or you are confident they will be overcome. Or if your scores are high but not high enough, how can you make the difference? What quality and characteristic can you give yourself more of?

Conversations with others:

Same people – improved conversations?

Achieving a Conversation with Impact does not necessarily mean having to change who you are talking to. If you know that your existing conversations are not Conversations with Impact, but feel they have the potential to be, look back over their individual scores and use the questionnaire to see what can potentially turn them into Conversations with Impact.

Ask yourself:

- what you need someone to keep giving you
- what you need them to give more of
- what would make them a Conversation with Impact.

Share the findings of your questionnaire with the person or people concerned. They are clearly important to you in some way and involving them provides an opportunity for them to focus more on the qualities and characteristics you need. All I will say is think carefully about approaching someone and how you will do so. Even though you value their conversation, are they people you can talk to about this—or not? If they are and they agree to give you what you need, you can assess whether your new conversations with them are making the difference you are after. If you decide not to ask them, then that's ok. You can continue to benefit from the relationship knowing that you need to find someone else.

Important people – low scores?

What if a low score applies to someone <u>really</u> important to you in some way? If it's someone that you have to talk to? As a coach and therapist, I am very aware that we can't always change our partner or boss even if we wanted to. When it comes to such conversations, you have to be kind to yourself. You have to be selfish in a good way by asking if:

- you have the ability or inclination to talk to them about what you need
- they are someone who will be receptive to changing how they talk to you.

If you decide not to try and change such a conversation for the better, then it is important to see this positively. It can be easy to feel guilty, deceitful or even ashamed because you lack the courage. Please don't. Remember, if you have difficulties and challenges and this person can't or won't help, you have every right to seek out someone who can and will.

It might be that an outcome of finding someone new who can give you a Conversation with Impact is an increase in your self-confidence. As a result you might decide to go back to the <u>really</u> important person concerned to ask them for an improved conversation. If they are amenable to this, then great. If they are not, then you have every right to consider whether this person needs to remain a part of your life.

"My husband used to criticise me for lacking ambition. My attempts to get him to understand that I just had different ambitions to him, were always rejected. Completing the questionnaire showed me what my husband wasn't giving me: unconditional support. I showed him the questionnaire I did for our conversations. He apologised and decided to support me." Nina

Need to talk to someone new?

If completing my questionnaires makes it clear you need someone new to talk to, then here are some points to consider. Whoever you find, explain the reason you are talking to them is because your existing conversations are not making the difference you are after. Show them your questionnaires and scores. Be specific about the characteristics and qualities you are looking for. If they can provide them, then great. If they can't, then no hard feelings. Finding the right person is important and what is important is worth taking the time for.

Remember. This book is about overcoming your difficulties and succeeding at your challenges. The person you choose needs to be someone who gives you a Conversation with Impact because only one of these can take you through every stage of the IMPACT model.

What to talk about?

If you do decide to find someone new to talk to, the next step is deciding what to talk to them about. And this gives me the chance to introduce the list of areas that will feature throughout this book. These are the significant areas where all of our difficulties and challenges are to be found in life, areas my IMPACT Model has been designed for.

To get you started, think about your most and least important areas by using a 0-10 scale (10 equals very important, 0 equals no importance).

- yourself
- relationships – personal and/or professional
- mental and physical health, psychological health
- emotional and physical wellbeing
- education, work or career
- personal and professional transformation
- social and cultural issues
- significant events
- past, present and future
- lifestyle issues.

The aim of this chapter and my questionnaires is to be diagnostic. Looking at your priority areas, what clues do they offer about who you need to talk to? For example, if you want to work on your Professional Transformation, look for someone who can support you professionally such as a coach or careers consultant. Or if you are living with past traumas, choose someone experienced in this field such as a trauma therapist. There is no point choosing someone who can't give you what you need.

If you don't know who to talk to or what to talk about but recognise the need to do so, explain this to whoever you do approach. Coaches and therapists like me are used to people who don't know where to start. If we can help you then great but if not, we will have a good idea of who can.

How to have a Conversation with Impact

The 'how' can happen as soon as you reflect on the outcomes of your own questionnaire and share the outcomes of the other questionnaire with the person (or people) you have decided to talk to. As you work through this book, make a commitment to focusing on the qualities and characteristics you need from your conversations to make the difference you are after. Assess the progress you make as you work through the remaining 5 stages. If you get stuck, use the questionnaires to find out what explains your 'stuck-ness.' Consider how you and/or the other people you are talking to can make the difference you are after by finding more of the qualities and characteristics you need.

Finally, expect fluctuations in how important your own conversations and those with other people are to you. In other words, notice when you need to talk more or less with yourself, and more or less with other people.

What stops people from having a 'Conversation with Impact?'

The simple answer is often people don't know that their conversations are the issue in the first place. Or if they have some idea, they don't know why they aren't helping because they don't know what is missing from them and have no way of finding out. And a final issue is that the people they are talking to don't know how to give them the conversation they need, or worse don't want to.

Summary of Chapter One

- Persistent difficulties and challenges are the result of conversations that are missing important qualities and characteristics, which mean they can never make the difference we are after.
- Conversations with Impact become possible when we are able to identify what qualities and characteristics are missing from our existing conversations.
- The Conversations with Impact questionnaires can help us to change how we talk to ourselves and to the people we already know, and they can also help us to decide if we need to talk to someone new.

"I attended a workshop run by Mark and was really struck by the idea that I had never thought about whether my conversations were helpful or not. The biggest change has been in my relationship with my 18-year-old son. He told me he found it difficult to open up to me about his anxiety. He completed a questionnaire for our conversations and it showed me that I try to fix things and take control of his life, whereas what he needed from me was to listen and ask how I can support him." Sarah

Bridge of curiosity

Where you are now is not where you want to be. Where you want to be is somewhere else, but your difficulty is you don't know where that somewhere else is or how to get there. You know you have to get to where you want to be because staying where you are isn't an option. As you ponder your predicament, a bridge appears in front of you. While you can't see over to the other side, you have a sixth sense that stepping on to it is the right thing to do. You notice the bridge is made of stone and etched into the stone on the right side is what you assume to be its name – 'The Bridge of Curiosity'. And then you notice that the bridge is etched with other writings, all in the form of questions.

'Why do you need to get to the other side?'

'What do you not have or know that will get you to the other side?'

'Who can show you how to get across?'

'Who will you be over the other side?'

The more you look, the more questions you see. And the more you see, the curiouser you become. And the curiouser you become, the more of the bridge you see up ahead. "Now that is curious," you say to yourself. An idea pops into your head. You look away from the questions and stop being curious. "Yes," you say, "I knew it!" For up ahead the bridge seems to disappear into nothingness. You have no choice. Only curiosity will get you over to the other side and where you want to be. And so you let your curiosity get to work, helped along by the questions carved into the stonework of the bridge.

Just as suddenly as one side of the Bridge of Curiosity

appeared, so does the other side. Looking straight ahead you take in the landscape opening up in front of you. Your attention is drawn to a sign that removes any doubt about what you are seeing. It says, 'Where you want to be.' As you reach the end of the bridge, you notice a hammer and chisel resting against its righthand side. Picking them up, you chisel a question of your own into the stone. Then you step off.

M is for Meaning

"As silly as it sounds, I found myself shouting at my dogs. Whenever it was walkies they would go nuts with excitement—because they're dogs. But this would really, really get me angry. I mean I would go ballistic. It was only when my wife admitted that I was scaring her that I did something about it. What I came to realise was I needed life to be just so, for people, my dogs and life to do as they're told, to tow the line. And then the penny dropped. My anger was linked to control. I am not joking when I say my whole life suddenly made sense." Duncan

The need for meaning brings two types of people together. Those in need of meaning and those who help them find it. My professions—therapy and coaching—are just two that help with the finding of meaning. Meaning is a stage in the IMPACT model because in its various forms, it can make the difference between paralysis and progress in life.

In this chapter, I consider meaning in the following way:

To understand why things are as they are

I realise there is a great deal more to the topic of meaning, such as meaning something to ourselves and other people and to lead a meaningful life, but these are addressed more generally by the whole book.

Why things are as they are

Often what motivates someone to contact me or to pick up a book like this, is because they are unable to understand—make sense of—why things are as they are. Someone might know they are stuck or in difficulty, but the 'why' is shrouded in mystery.

What do I mean by 'things?' I mean anything someone has become aware of that is difficult or challenging in some way. Examples include:

- intrusive thoughts, unsettling feelings or unpleasant physical symptoms
- harmful or destructive behaviours such as obsessions, compulsions or addictions
- emotional states such as stress, anxiety and depression
- self-esteem and confidence
- identity and sexuality
- social and cultural factors
- difficulties in important areas of life such as family, relationships and work
- difficulty making progress in life personally and/or professionally

- a life that lacks meaning and purpose
- a combination of the above.

Making sense

I see 'making sense of,' as the active process by which someone seeks to explain the existence and presence of some or all of the above 'things,' which they have become aware of to greater or lesser degrees. Sense-making can be a solo effort when we are alone with our thoughts. It can be a shared experience when we seek answers from others. And it can involve gathering information from books and websites, film and television.

An inability to make sense of our experiences makes it hard to articulate what we are going through both to ourselves and to others. How many of us when asked by a partner or friend "What is wrong? What is the matter?" have replied, "I don't know." Human beings are a sense-making species and our ability to thrive and survive depends on this ability. While we don't always need an exact explanation (even if one can sometimes be extremely helpful) we do need to make enough sense of our difficulties and challenges if we are to resolve and overcome them.

"My mental health was shocking throughout my teens. Working through a timeline of my life, when I reached 13 years old, I remembered someone tried to sexually assault me on a family holiday. I was fine before I was 13. No one had ever linked my mental health to that event even though they knew about it. Years of GP visits and therapy and all I needed was for someone to make sense of that experience for me." Lucy

An emotional mystery

Being unable to make sense of why things are, as they are, generates emotions such as stress and anxiety. Such emotions are how our mind/body system complains when it notices we haven't a clue what is going on when we really need to. Being in a state of mystery or ignorance sets in motion a vicious circle. For example:

- stress caused by our difficulties and challenges
- stress caused by our inability to make sense of them
- stress caused by the resulting deterioration in our quality of life

Looking in the wrong place

Understandably, there can be an energy-sapping focus on what is known, the effects and symptoms of our difficulties. These come in a variety of different forms and are often the catalyst for people to act or for others to comment on. Some common examples include:

- physical symptoms such as chest pain and headaches
- negative, intrusive thoughts
- problematic behaviours such as procrastination and over-indulgence (eating, drinking, drug-taking etc.)
- difficult emotions such as anxiety, depression and anger
- relationship issues such as irritability and intolerance.

A focus on effects and symptoms is understandable, especially as they can be highly distressing, but doing so will only prove effective if they can be made sense of. If they can't be, then the person struggling and anyone else they are talking to *are looking in the wrong place.* How do you know if you are looking in the wrong place? Because effects and symptoms persist and worsen.

Looking in the right place

I worked with a severely depressed university student who I shall call Tim. Sitting in front of me, his head was hung low, his eyes staring at the floor. In the final year of an accountancy degree, Tim was very concerned that his mental health would make it hard for him to graduate. It quickly emerged that his depression was a mystery to him and despite some initial exploration it remained this way. However, something didn't add up for me. Here was an accountancy student wearing a Sex Pistols t-shirt, a leather jacket, black skinny jeans and a hairstyle like Johnny Rotten. I had worked with many accountancy students and he looked like none of them. I leant forward to gain eye contact with Tim and asked, "Why are you studying accountancy?"

He looked up and replied, "I don't know."

"If you don't mind me saying," I continued, "you don't look like a typical accountancy student."

"I hate it," he said. "I'm only here because of my family—to make them proud."

I asked him what he would rather be doing. "Playing in my band back in Hartlepool with my mates. We're pretty good and want to give ourselves a chance." And there it was: meaning. "Is that why I am depressed?" he asked. "Yes, I think it probably is," I replied. I saw Tim for two further

23

sessions. He was transformed. That summer I received an email from him.

> "Hi Mark—thought you would like to know. I graduated with a 2:1 and am midway through a tour with my band. My family are truly proud of me. I want you to know the difference you made in helping me make sense of my depression. It released something, and I will never forget that feeling." Tim

Tim spent three years looking in the wrong place. GP visits, different antidepressant medications, conversations with family and friends, practical help from his university tutors—none of which brought any clarity. So, how do we know where the right place to look is? The answer to this question will be found somewhere within this chapter and my IMPACT model.

Finding the right place: emotions as messages

When it comes to 'making sense' of why things are as they are, emotions are a great guide. I have always subscribed to the idea that emotions are messages, a form of communication containing vital information to help us thrive and survive. As a practitioner, I encourage my clients to respond to their emotions like any other important message: make sure it is received, made sense of and responded to. In this section I will show you how you can make this idea work for you.

Difficult emotions such as stress, anxiety, depression and anger contain messages indicating our ability to thrive and survive is being threatened or hampered in some way. The opposite message is conveyed by positive emotions.

Introducing your Emotional Self

If emotions are messages, then who is the sender? Let me introduce you to your Emotional Self. I have worked with thousands of clients over the years and this has proven to be one of my most effective concepts. People quickly grasp the idea of an 'Emotional Self,' who is sending messages because sending and receiving messages is a normal part of our daily lives. When we feel an emotion, we are being invited into a conversation or dialogue with our 'Emotional Self.' Once this is understood we can become active participants in some of the most significant conversations we will ever have.

It is important to understand your Emotional Self is ALWAYS trying to be helpful.

After all, its job IS to help us thrive and survive. With positive emotions, it is easy to think of a helpful Emotional Self, but with difficult emotions like severe stress, anxiety or depression? How is that being helpful? I accept this is a tough sell. You won't need me to tell you about the adverse effects that difficult emotions such as depression can have on people's lives. They remind us something is wrong while often taking away our ability to do anything about it. Again, how is that being helpful?

When it comes to difficult emotions, I am encouraging you to look beyond the effects and symptoms to their purpose to help us thrive and survive. Human beings do not experience these emotions for no reason. There will be an explanation and there will be something that can be done to help most people. Therefore, it is vital that we befriend our Emotional Self. Yes, they might deliver really important messages in really unhelpful ways, but an Emotional Self that feels listened to is an Emotional Self that will be kind to us in return.

There are two important parts to our emotional messages that our Emotional Self wants us to know about. The first part is about the causes of our emotions. These can be internal or external to us—or both.

Examples of internal causes of difficult emotions include:

- low self-esteem because it is often characterised by self-critical thoughts and self-sabotaging behaviours, which make thriving and surviving hard if not impossible. The message from the Emotional Self is, "Please increase your self-esteem and positively change how you think and behave."
- trauma (and its symptoms such as flashbacks) because it can severely hinder someone's ability to function and live a normal life. Again, the message from the Emotional Self is the same: "Please resolve your trauma, function effectively and live a normal life."

Examples of external causes of difficult emotions include:

- insecure employment, which can undermine the need for security and control, or living in a threatening, and unsafe environment. Message? "Please do something about your employment status," or, "Please make your environment safe or move to one that is."

This part of the message is plain and simple:

- difficult emotions: something is wrong, please do something about it
- positive emotions: something is right, please continue.

The second part of the message indicates how near or far our Emotional Selves think we are from overcoming the causes so we can thrive and survive. The further away our Emotional Selves think we are, the more intense and difficult the emotion. The closer we are, the more intense and positive the emotion.

Our Emotional Self takes its role very seriously and is determined to carry it out at any cost because our thriving and surviving is so important. If there is one thing our Emotional Selves hate more than anything it is being ignored. In fact, they hate it so much that being ignored simply makes them dig their heels in. What they want, and are determined to get, is us—their owner—in conversation. Our Emotional Selves WILL NOT STOP until its message is delivered, made sense of, and responded to. If you want to fully appreciate how loud and determined our Emotional Selves can get, you only need to look at the severe end of the mental health spectrum.

A failure to communicate

The problem though, is that the way our Emotional Selves communicate isn't very effective; they can't talk to us; they can't email, text or direct message us. All they have at their disposal is emotion, which they increase or decrease depending on whether they are getting their message through. Our Emotional Selves are reliant on us knowing we are being communicated with in the first place, and then on our ability to effectively translate and make sense of the emotional messages it sends. If we don't know, then we're in trouble until we do. And this is where books like this can play a vital role: helping you make sense of why things are as they are.

What are YOUR messages about?

Now you know you have an Emotional Self and it is trying to get an important message through; the next step is to identify what your messages are about. But wait a minute, I hear you ask. How does my Emotional Self know to send messages in the first place? And then to know which messages to send? Great questions (once asked by an old client of mine called William). The answers can be found by looking at the many functions of our mind/body systems. Some of its functions have to do with monitoring, assessment and oversight, and what is being monitored, assessed and overseen is the degree to which you are thriving and surviving. All of your messages are about thriving and surviving because ultimately nothing else matters.

Below are some familiar areas we all want to get right in life so we can thrive and survive. In the box next to the list and using a 0-10 scale, indicate whether you feel an area is causing you difficulties and challenges or not. 0 indicates an area is very positive for you, 10 means the opposite. As a general rule:

- any area scored 6 or above is likely to be problematic or very problematic
- any area scored 4 or 5 is likely to be neither good nor bad

- any area scored 3 or below is likely to be positive or very positive.

Think about the emotions you are experiencing on a regular or even permanent basis, which you now know are messages from your Emotional Self:

Are they positive messages or not?

Does your Emotional Self like what it is seeing?

Or is it concerned?

Area	Score	Positive, neither good nor bad, problematic
Yourself		
Family		
Environment		
Education		
Work and Career		
Money		
Relationships		
Social and Cultural		
Wellbeing		
Lifestyle		

Delivered, made sense of, and responded to.

The aim of this exercise is to encourage you to communicate with your Emotional Self. We want IT to know ITS message has been delivered and you have started to make sense of it by connecting your emotions to your scores. And we want IT to know you will be responding appropriately by:

- maintaining any 0-3 scores
- improving if necessary, any 4 or 5 scores
- demonstrating a serious commitment to improve any 6+ scores.

By communicating with your Emotional Self in this way, you are telling it what it wants to hear, and that you are starting to make sense of why things are as they are. Don't worry too much at this stage what your response is going to be because that is the purpose of the whole book. For now, I want to you to develop and deepen the relationship with your Emotional Self. Let it know you understand its two-part message:

- internal and/or external causes of your emotions
- how near or far you are from thriving and surviving.

Emotions as messages: past, present and future

Another way to make sense of why things are as they are, is to think of emotional messages from a time perspective. Human beings exist in time and who we are and what we do is characterised by it. Our brains can be thought of as time machines that are geared up to operate simultaneously in our past, present and future.

A consistent positive emotional state albeit with the usual

ups and downs is our Emotional Self's way of communicating that it likes how we are aligning our past, present and future. Alignment means carrying forth what has worked from our past and letting go of what hasn't; making the best of our present while having a positive, flexible plan with regards to our future. A consistent negative emotional state, therefore, is how our Emotional Self communicates that it doesn't like what it sees when it comes to our past, present and future alignment.

The past, present and future may all be relevant, but to make sense of why things are as they are, we need to work out the relative influence of each of them. Only when we know this can we begin to make the positive changes that will bring our past, present and future into alignment.

> "Even at primary school I knew I would be the one who wouldn't go to university. From a young age I saw myself as stupid and incapable of doing well. My past had dictated my entire life. With this understanding, I changed my present view of myself. I am now a trainee accountant with a future to look forward to. Not bad for someone who left school and college with nothing. I look back at my young self with compassion and empathy, knowing they got themselves wrong." Faisal

It doesn't always follow that past issues require a past focus, or future issues a future one. This is because making positive changes in one area can result in positive changes to the others automatically. Faisal's moving testimonial is an example of someone's past and future being improved by mainly working on their present. Our Emotional Self will let us know if we are working in the right areas or not. It will assess whether we are helping or hindering our ability to thrive and survive and send the appropriate form of emotional message. As a coach and therapist, I take my lead from my clients' emotional messages in helping them achieve the right focus between their past, present and future. If the messages are negative, I know the balance isn't right; if they are positive, I know it is.

Past, present and future: areas to consider.

Below is the list of areas from page 29. You can see I have added a column for past, present and future. In this column indicate as appropriate.

Area	Score	Positive, neither good nor bad, problematic	Is the area past, present or future?
Yourself			
Family			
Environment			
Education			
Work and Career			
Money			
Relationships			

Social and Cultural			
Wellbeing			
Lifestyle			

Identifying the influence of your past, present and future further reassures your Emotional Self that you are on your way to making sense of why things are as they are.

A coherent narrative

When it comes to making sense of why things are as they are, having a coherent or clear narrative that captures key details of our past, present and future can be really helpful. This is because it reduces the guess work involved as we seek to understand our difficulties and challenges. Without one we are left with only effects and symptoms to work things out with, which as I have suggested can be diagnostically unreliable. The client stories featured in this chapter are testament to the power of a coherent narrative to help people find meaning and make sense of their lives.

A coherent narrative will typically be made up of specific details, plus broader themes, such as:

- memories
- the key people in our lives and their influence on us
- significant events and happenings
- important periods such as our early years, schooling, teens and stages in our adult life

- general life patterns such as achievements or setbacks, positive or negative relationships, good or poor levels of self-esteem and self-worth.

All of the above can make a valuable contribution in putting together a coherent narrative. In my experience there isn't an ideal mix of specific details and general themes that is required to make sense of why things are as they are. In other words, don't get caught up in a potentially futile search for the one memory or event—it might not exist. Looking back at the table on page 32–3, can you build your own narrative? If you can't, then think about who you can speak to who can help. Use the questionnaires introduced in chapter one to help you find the right person.

Vicki came to see me for severe anxiety. The trigger for her anxiety was being alone. So bad had this issue become that she would wait in a local café for her partner and mum, with whom she lived, to get home from work before going home herself. She was at a loss to explain why being alone was so difficult for her. After some investigation, she recalled a difficult childhood. Her father left her and her mother one day without warning, never to be seen or heard from again. Her mum, saddled with huge debts run up by her father, was forced to work two jobs and through necessity Vicki was left alone a lot of the time. Making the connection between her past and present circumstances resolved the issue for her.

Observing self

During my therapy training, I read a book by American psychiatrist Arthur Deikman, called The Observing Self. The book is an exploration of what modern psychological practice can learn from how ancient, mystical traditions approached psychological healing. *The Observing Self* is one concept from these traditions and the basis to Deikman's book.

Who or what is The Observing Self? Well, we all have one, and my understanding is that The Observing Self is the same as our 'real' or 'core' self. It's you and me, 'The Chief,' 'The Boss' and 'Decision Maker.' It is the part of us who oversees our lives and everything in them, who steps back, reflects on how we want things to be and who sets things in motion. Your Observing Self is the part of you who found this book and the part of you who will finish it. In other words, your Observing Self is YOU. And who are you? You are the person who wants to thrive and survive and to put your difficulties and challenges behind you.

When we struggle in life and fall into a cycle of negative thinking, behaving, feeling and relating, we can make sense of this by understanding that our Observing Self is no longer in charge. In this section I will show you who does take charge during difficult periods and why they are responsible for why things are as they are.

Making sense of your difficulties and challenges

On page 38 is an illustration of my Observing Self model. In the middle is your Observing Self and around them are what I call your sub-selves, who play specific roles in your life. Your sub-selves are a part of you, but they are NOT who you are. As you will see, this distinction is crucial. The purpose of your Observing Self is to create harmony between your sub-selves and to ensure they are fully supportive of you.

What should happen is this; your Observing Self, who is The Boss, remember, brings on a sub-self to play an appropriate role, temporarily relinquishing control to them. When the chosen sub-self has done its job, your Observing Self sends them back to the periphery of your life and takes charge again. So far so good. However, sometimes it doesn't work out this way.

Introducing your 'Negative Self'

Let me give you a scenario. One day during a difficult time in your life, one of your sub-selves, who I shall call your 'Negative Self' (sub-self A. in my illustration), was brought on to play a role, but when the time came for them to return to where they came from, they refused. They were enjoying being in charge far too much and try as your Observing Self did that day, they lost out and it was they who ended up on the periphery of your life. From that day onwards your Negative Self took control of how you think, feel and behave. They also took control of your relationships with the outside world and the people in it.

On page 22 in 'Looking in the wrong place' I listed the effects and symptoms we can experience in difficult and challenging periods.

No one chooses to inflict such misery on themselves, and yet for many people it is a daily reality made worse by an inability to make sense of it. This is where my Observing Self model comes in. It hands responsibility for these miserable effects and symptoms to your Negative Self.

As a practitioner, it is vital I demonstrate to a client they are NOT their Negative Self. Achieving this separation allows them to take back control of their own thoughts, behaviours, emotions and relationships—how do I show someone they are not their Negative Self? I simply refer to their presence in my practice room. Negative Selves don't book coaching or therapy sessions—or buy self-help books for that matter either. The thing about Negative Selves is they like the dominant role they play in someone's life—and they never act against their own interests. People like me and books like this represent a direct threat to their dominance. They didn't buy this book, you did. They aren't still reading, you are. And they aren't the ones wanting to thrive and survive... you get the idea.

The Observing Self activity

My Observing Self activity will show how your Negative Self has been hindering your ability to overcome your difficulties and achieve your challenges.

The illustration shows your Observing Self in the middle surrounded by your sub-selves, including your Negative Self (Self A). Notice they all have different facial expressions. This is to help you decide which part of you they represent or can represent. I have included 6 sub-selves, but you can have as many or as few as you like. As you are looking to regain control of your life from your Negative Self, ideally you want a group of positive sub-selves who will support you in this.

Between your Observing Self and your sub-selves are the mental bridges that your sub-selves cross when they are required. It is this bridge that your Negative Self refused to go back across when they took over. When I do this activity with people, they are often surprised by the existence of sub-selves who can and will support them. Only then do they realise how effective their Negative Self has been in hiding them from view.

Now you have been reintroduced to all of your sub-selves, the next stage is to give each of them their own name, personality and role in your life. In other words, bring them to life. Do this for your Negative Self as well, but this time it will be you telling them who they are and not the other way around. When choosing roles for your 'rediscovered' positive sub-selves, make sure they support your commitment to thriving and surviving. The list below is from one of my clients to act as a guide, but bring them all to life in ways that truly reflect who you are.

A.   Negative Self.
B.   Optimistic Self.
C.   Compassionate Self.
D.   Helpful Self.
E.   Determined & Resilient Self.

'F' is a separate sub-self from the rest and is dotted deliberately. 'F' is your future self and it is dotted because you are always becoming it without ever actually being it. 'F' is important because as you get older it takes on the personalities and roles of your Observing Self and other sub-selves. This is why it is so important to separate from your Negative Self because if you don't, it will ensure 'F'— your future self—simply gets more negative as you age. With your Observing Self in charge and supported by your positive sub-selves, 'F' can become who you want it to be.

Taking each sub-self, complete the following:

- my Negative Self got me to

    · think like this
    · behave like this
    · feel like this
    · relate like this

- My sub-self B is called X and they

    · think like this
    · behave like this
    · feel like this
    · relate like this

- All other sub-selves C, D and E are called, and they

    · think like this

- behave like this
- feel like this
- relate like this

• My Observing Self is me, and I now

- think like this
- behave like this
- feel like this
- relate like this

• My Future self F is called, and they will

- think like this
- behave like this
- feel like this
- relate like this

What did you discover?

"Even though I was in a senior leadership position in charge of 100 or so people, the tag of 'imposter' was never far away. No matter how well I progressed professionally, I could hear that voice in my head telling me I was a fraud and didn't deserve to be here. For all of my life I believed that voice. And then there it was beautifully, simply expressed: tricked into believing I was an imposter by my negative self. I have done loads of leadership training, but this exercise nailed it for me." Karen

My hope is that the activity put YOU back in charge and brought back into your life a group of sub-selves that will play a role in helping you to achieve your transformation.

A note of caution. Negative Selves rarely appreciate being

sent back to the periphery of our lives. So expect them to kick up a stink and make it hard for you. Anticipate they will try to regain control of your life by trying everything at their disposal. Remember, they succeeded once, so they will feel confident about doing so again. The difference this time around is you will be ready for them. From now on whenever you think, behave, feel and relate negatively, you will know this is your Negative Self looking to regain lost ground. By using my IMPACT model and drawing on your own strengths and resources, you can outwit them by being smarter and more determined. Repeat the activity from time to time to ensure you remain on track and in control of your life.

The Valuables Test

People give away their most valuable possession away when their negative self tricks them into engaging in self-sabotaging thoughts and behaviours, their health and wellbeing. And yet if someone were asked to hand over everything of value they possess by a complete stranger, the answer would be, "no!" Their house, car, money, technology or things of emotional value – none of it would they give away. And yet when their negative self comes along and asks them to hand over their value, they do so without question.

So why would someone fight to hold on to their laptop and family photos, but not their health and wellbeing? How does their negative self persuade them to hand over, often without a fight, the very thing on which everything else depends?

What if you stopped giving away what you value to your negative self? How would that come about? It could go something like this:

Start by listing everything of value you possess. Once you have your list, really connect with the possessions on it. Remind yourself what they mean to you. Now imagine a stranger or even someone you really don't like asking you to hand it all over. How do you feel? I hope you feel like saying, "no."

Now locate in your mind and body where that, "no" resides. This is your 'place of certainty'. When your negative self comes along, which it will, and asks you to hand over everything of value again, be ready for it. Locate your 'place of certainty' and stare it in the face. It wants nothing more than to take away what you value the most. This time you will say "no."

Summary of Chapter Two

- To get beyond our difficulties and challenges, we have to be able to make sense of why things are as they are.
- The best source of meaning is our emotions, which contain messages from our Emotional Self. These messages are all about our thriving and surviving and how we feel about the main areas of our lives.
- Understanding the influence of our past, present and future is important in helping us make sense of our experiences, as is having a coherent narrative of our lives.
- The Observing Self idea can help us make sense of negative ways of thinking, behaving, feeling and relating.
- The Valuables Test can ensure we value ourselves and learn to keep hold of what we value the most: our health and wellbeing

P is for Patterns

Here are two scenarios

Scenario One

I am looking at your difficulties and challenges under a microscope. What do I see? Initially I see the rough outline of a pattern. Then as my eyes adjust and take in more detail, I see what the pattern consists of. I see separate, but interwoven patterns, including patterns of thought, behaviour, feelings and relationships. Lifting my head from over the microscope, I engage you in conversation.

"What am I seeing?" I ask you.

"Oh, that's what I always do. It's just who I am. I'd rather do things differently, be a different version of myself, but somehow it never works out that way."

"But if it did work out that way," I persist, "what might I see?"

"Well," you say, "you would see a different set of patterns."

Scenario Two

I am looking at your difficulties and challenges under a microscope. What do I see? Initially I see the rough outline of a pattern. Then as my eyes adjust and take in more detail, I see what the pattern consists of. I see separate, but interwoven patterns, including patterns of thought, behaviour, feelings and relationships. Lifting my head from over the microscope, I engage you in conversation.

"What am I seeing?" I ask you.

"Oh, that's what I always do. It's just who I am. I'm always looking to tweak and improve, fine tune and strengthen."

"Great," I reply. "If I come back in six months? What might I see then?"

"Well," you say, "you would see a new and improved set of patterns."

In this chapter, my aims are to help you to:

- develop your understanding of what patterns are and the types that exist
- identify the unhelpful patterns in your life and how you can replace them
- identify the helpful patterns in your life that you wish to develop further.

To get you started, I am going to tell you a story called The Cliff Edge. I use stories a lot in my work, and The Cliff Edge is one that seems to resonate with people more than most. Perhaps it is the visual nature of the story and its ability to engage the imagination? All I know is that it frequently produces valuable insight and awareness. Therefore you might want to engineer some privacy for yourself by finding a quiet space free from interruptions. Take a pen and paper, too, so you can note down what the story triggers for you.

The 'Cliff Edge.'

You find yourself in an unfamiliar place. Although you try to get your bearings, the dense fog that surrounds you makes this impossible. So thick is the fog, in fact, that when you put your hand up to your face, you can't see your hand. You stumble along when all of a sudden, the ground disappears from beneath your feet and you fall into nothingness. Seconds pass and still you are falling—you assume from a great height. Thump! You hit the ground. Coming to, you are bumped and bruised, but it appears no real damage is done.

Lying flat on the ground, you look up and reflect on what just happened. You decide not to give yourself a hard time because you had never been to that place before and the fog made it doubly difficult; one of those unfortunate incidents.

The following day, you are back in the same place although you don't know this yet. Today it is clear and sunny, and you can see for miles in every direction. Although this place looks unfamiliar—you don't recognise any part of the landscape—you have a gut feeling that you have been here before. Walking for a short while, you notice something up ahead. As you get closer, what you see is a cliff edge! The penny drops and your gut instinct makes sense. "Ah!" you exclaim. This is where you were yesterday, when the ground disappeared beneath your feet.

A few seconds later you hit the ground with a thump. It takes you a while to figure out what happened, but only one conclusion presents itself: you went over the cliff edge again. This time your reflections are altogether different. While yesterday you can understand why you went over, today it does not make sense at all. After all, you saw the cliff edge before you got to it and yet for reasons best known to yourself, over you went. The bumps and bruises are more severe this time and the forgiving tone of yesterday has been replaced by something far more critical. In fact, you give yourself a hard time.

Next day and you are back. There is something very seductive about this place, something that is drawing you back. You know exactly where you are, of course. Up ahead is the cliff edge. Suddenly your brain registers that your right foot is no longer in contact with the ground. Adrenaline rushes through your body and you throw yourself backwards, landing with much less of a thump a metre or so away from the cliff edge. "Phew! That was close," you say.

The awareness of what you have just prevented begins to register with you. "If I am to return to this place, and I accept that I must, I can't keep going over that cliff edge." You give it another glance and shake your head. Getting to your feet your gaze takes in the panorama of the landscape—a beautiful landscape. A question comes to mind. If I am not going over the cliff, then where am I going? Your gaze sweeps the landscape again and it settles on a spot not too far away. An intense feeling, more intense than the one that kept bringing you back to the cliff edge, connects itself to the spot not too far away. It is a feeling of hope and potential.

"I'm going OVER THERE," you say to yourself. Mentally, you trace a path from where you are now to where you want to be. A few seconds later you are on that path. The cliff edge still exerts its influence and you feel its pull at times, but like a fraying rope at breaking point, it becomes a weak tether. The further down the path you travel, the stronger the pull of 'over there' becomes. And then it dawns on you in a moment of true liberation that you will never go over that cliff edge again.

What is a 'cliff edge?'

A cliff edge is anything we do a lot of that isn't working.

What is 'over there?'

Over there is where we do a lot of that is working. It is the place we go to when we are not going over our cliff edges, where we are who we want to be and doing what we want to be doing.

What is a pattern?

From the perspective of my IMPACT model, a pattern is anything that features regularly in our lives that positively or negatively contributes to thriving and surviving. A pattern can be thought of as being internal to us, such as patterns of thought, or external to us, such as patterns of relationships. Usually patterns will have both internal and external characteristics such as when we think of someone or something else.

How do patterns form?

Patterns that form in our lives are a combination of innate (what we are born with—nature) and learnt patterns (what we learn from others and by ourselves—nurture). Take language. Nature gives us a head start and then we build on it through nurture. Sometimes this process works to our advantage and sometimes the opposite is true. Understanding how to encourage the former and avoid the latter is the subject of this chapter.

Unhelpful patterns form for positive reasons

It will not come as a surprise to you to discover that helpful patterns start for positive reasons. What might surprise you is that unhelpful patterns start for positive reasons, too. I want this to be your working assumption: an unhelpful pattern, one that has become established in your life, will have started for a positive reason i.e. as something that helped you and made enough of a difference at a particular time in your life. A common example is overeating to cope with stress or unhappiness. In this chapter, we will look at how to resolve this contradiction, but for now I will leave you with this thought: while a part of you might know if a pattern is harmful, another part might not know or even care. Which parts of you, I hear you ask? Well, you have already been introduced to them. Your Observing Self and your sub-selves. Guess which part of you doesn't care? Guess which part of you lays down and reinforces unhelpful patterns? Your negative self.

Awareness

Awareness is key. If we are unaware of a pattern, then we might think there is nothing to change or improve! Or we might mistake partial for complete awareness and fail to see enough of a pattern. And as we saw in chapter two on Meaning, the less we know about matters of importance, the more our Emotional Selves make their presence known. Like a light being turned on in the darkness, awareness allows us to have a good look at our patterns and to ask important questions, such as:

- what am I doing a lot of that isn't working?
- what am I not doing enough of that is?
- what am I doing that I need to stop or do much less of?
- what am I doing that is working and that I can build and develop?

The aim of this chapter is to increase your awareness so you can both answer these questions and act on them.

Types of patterns

Below are the main types of patterns I come across in my work. Have a look at the list and consider my questions, adding any of your own as you do so. Make a mental note of any thoughts or observations as we will come back to this list later in the chapter. Remember to keep my definition of a pattern (page 48) in mind in deciding what your patterns are.

- Attention: what do you focus your attention on?
- Thoughts: how would you describe your style of thinking?
- Time: what is your relationship like with the past, present and future?
- Beliefs: what do you believe about yourself and the world around you?
- Behaviours: what do you do most often? What are your routines?
- Emotions/feelings: what do you know about your feelings and emotions?
- Relationships: what types of relationships do you form with:

- · people
- · places and spaces
- · objects/things.

- Physical movements, postures: how do you express yourself physically?
- Academia/education and professional/work/ career: how do you go about this?

Doing, causing and occurring patterns

A second way I think of pattern types is in terms of doing, causing and occurring. Doing and causing patterns I see as:

- anything someone does or causes regularly that is either helpful or unhelpful.

Occurring patterns I see as:

- anything occurring regularly to someone that is either helpful or unhelpful.

By labelling patterns in these two ways, I am distinguishing between patterns that someone knows they do or cause in some way—even if they don't know why—and those that happen or appear to happen to someone without explanation or even without them realising. The terms reflect my experience as a practitioner and break down into the following:

- patterns that someone knows they do or cause and why.
- patterns that someone knows they do or cause without knowing why.
- patterns that someone knows just occur without

- realising they play a role in doing or causing them.
- Patterns that someone is unaware of entirely.

"When my wife suggested I was eating too much, I took offence. So she got my jeans and suit trousers out from the wardrobe and told me to put them on. I couldn't. I remember bursting into tears. Then the real showstopper. My wife showed me a diary she had been keeping of my eating habits. When I saw Mark and we did some work on my patterns I was able to see my journey from total unawareness to fully knowing that I did and caused them, and importantly why – because I was unhappy." David

How someone sees their patterns is so important. If you know you do or cause your unhelpful patterns and why, it is much, much easier to interrupt and replace them with helpful ones. And if you know you do or cause your helpful patterns and why, it is much, much easier for existing ones to be strengthened and new ones laid down. In this chapter, I want you to get to where David did: to know you do or cause your unhelpful patterns and why.

What I know as a coach and therapist is that with occurring patterns we don't take credit for anything positive in our lives, and believe there is nothing we can do about anything negative. This is a real shame because we should, and we can.

Past, present and future patterns

A third way I think of patterns is from the perspective of our past, present and future. Although we experience our patterns in the present, when it comes to changing them it can be helpful to identify what part of our lives they relate to. For example, a trauma pattern might be connected to our past; a stress pattern connected to our present; and a fear pattern connected to our future. Once we know the past, present and future make-up of our patterns, we can ask some helpful questions:

- what past patterns do I want to bring with me and what do I want to leave behind?
- what present patterns are working well for me and need to be maintained or improved?
- what present patterns are not working well for me and need to be addressed?
- are there any emerging present patterns that if allowed to develop might prove problematic for me?
- are there any emerging present patterns that I like the look of which can be nurtured and encouraged?
- if I were to travel into my future, what patterns would I like to see?

How do you know if the patterns in your life are helpful or unhelpful?

In the previous chapter on Meaning, I introduced you to your Emotional Self and how it communicates with you through sending either difficult or positive emotions. Your Emotional Self is very interested in your patterns and whether they are consistent with you thriving and surviving. If they aren't, then your emotional messages will be difficult, indicating you have more unhelpful patterns than helpful ones. The opposite will be true, of course, if your patterns are consistent with you thriving and surviving. When it comes to your patterns, your Emotional Self needs you to understand:

- they exist in the first place

- whether they are helpful or unhelpful
- what their type is
- what you are going to do about them to ensure you're thriving and surviving e.g. replacing unhelpful patterns or reinforcing helpful ones?

The Cliff Edge activity: discovering your patterns

'The Cliff Edge' activity addresses the concerns of your Emotional Self by helping you really get to know your patterns. The point in my Cliff Edge story at which the activity fits in is when you jump back from the Cliff Edge and save yourself from yet another bruising landing. It is the point in the story when you become acutely aware that you can't keep repeating your unhelpful patterns and need to do more of the helpful ones.

In order to make the activity as helpful as possible, here are some suggestions for how to go about it:

- do the exercise more than once. It can take time to become helpfully aware of our patterns.
- consider the different areas of your life you think are relevant such as home, work and social
- do the exercise by yourself and, if possible, with trusted others. When choosing trusted others, think back to chapter one and anyone who can give you a Conversation With Impact. Can it be with someone you know, or does it need to be with someone you don't know?
- appreciate your findings regardless of what you discover! It doesn't matter if or how often you are going over your Cliff Edges. All that matters at this stage is that you become aware you are doing so.

Patterns	Unhelpful – your Cliff Edges	Helpful – over there	Do, cause, occur	Past, present, future
Where you focus your attention				
How you think and what you think of				
How you remember your memories/past				
Your beliefs about yourself, others and the world				
How you behave; your behaviours				
How you feel; your emotions/feelings				
Your relationships - people, places, objects				
Academic/educational and professional/work				

The Cliff Edge activity: what did you discover?

Have a look at the statements to help you reflect on your discoveries.

- The activity helped me realise I had no, or too little, awareness of the important patterns in my life.
- The activity revealed I have more unhelpful than helpful patterns in my life.
- The activity revealed I have more helpful than unhelpful patterns in my life.
- The activity helped me understand more about my pattern types.
- The activity has shown me what patterns I need to work on.
- I am still unsure what my important patterns are, but I know they must exist because my difficulties and challenges still persist.

Laying down helpful patterns

The Potter's Wheel and The Hammer

When we bring to mind a pattern and what it consists of, it is so important to think of it as something that can be reworked. A pattern is not like a painting on the wall that remains unchanged each time we look at it, but instead can be seen as a piece of clay on a potter's wheel waiting to be shaped and reshaped into something new. And if I give you a hammer, you can build something useful with it or hit yourself over the head. In other words, it is you, not the hammer, that produces the outcome. Laying down helpful patterns is a tool, like a hammer, that can be used positively or negatively.

Appreciating the importance of these two ideas cannot be underestimated. Hopefully, you will have a good idea of the helpful patterns you are looking to strengthen or start to lay down—the types and the areas of your life they relate to. So, let's get started.

Pattern matching

Pattern matching is a process whereby information coming in through our senses in the present, is 'pattern matched' to information we have already got stored 'up top' in our memory banks. This includes what we experience externally through sight, sound, touch, taste and smell, and what we experience internally through thoughts, feelings and physical sensations. Using pattern matching effectively can ensure you shape and reshape your piece of clay into something you like the look of, and build something beautiful with your hammer.

When new, emotionally significant information is pattern matched to similar stored information i.e. what we have experienced before, I want you to imagine your brain is asking itself various questions.

- What is this information, and what does it mean to my owner?
- What is this information, and what does it mean for my owner?
- What does my owner usually do with this information? How do they usually respond?
- This new information looks like this past information. Should I add the two together? Or should I reclassify the new information?

Once it has asked itself these questions, your brain turns to you for guidance. 'What should I do with this information?'

It is at this point that pattern matching becomes the most important process to both understand and make use of. This is because how we respond to our brain determines what happens next to our patterns. Take these three scenarios.

- **If we don't know the question is being asked, our brains take our silence as confirmation it can use our past as precedent. This results in existing patterns being reinforced.** Consider this scenario. Chris is struggling at work. Every time he comes to call a client, he has a panic attack. Simply looking at his phone is enough to trigger intense panic. What Chris doesn't know is that his brain is pattern matching each new client call to a disastrous one from a year ago, when he lost a major deal to a competitor. When he fails to respond, Chris' brain uses his past as precedent and runs the 'disaster' pattern, triggering a panic attack.

- **If we do know the question is being asked, but through our response confirm that nothing has changed, existing patterns are reinforced.** Let's return to Chris. Chris now knows that his brain is pattern matching each new client call to the disaster one from a year ago, but because his confidence is shot to pieces, he tells his brain nothing has changed since then. As a result, the disaster pattern is run, triggering a panic attack.

- **If we do know the question is being asked and through our response confirm that things have changed, existing patterns can be changed, and new ones laid down.** Back to Chris. It is a year after his disaster call. He walks into his office and warmly greets his colleagues. Sitting at his desk,

Chris looks at his phone, rehearses what he wants to say to an important client and calls them. Chris feels calm and confident and the call goes well. When Chris' brain asked the question 'What do you want me to do with this new information?' Chris responded by confirming that he had moved on from the disaster call and it was no longer relevant. Instead, Chris directed his brain to use the sales training he had undergone, the confidence coaching his manager had done with him and the successful deals he had achieved in recent months. As a result, his brain ran a calm and confident pattern.

Build a detailed picture

Changing how our brains pattern match so we can lay down new or improved patterns is made easier, when we have a detailed picture of the unhelpful patterns we want to change. Below are a series of 'pattern' questions that can help you to gather quality information about the patterns you need to replace or upgrade. I have included how Chris might have answered these questions as he sought to explain, understand and overcome his panic attacks.

A.   When, where and with whom were you when your unhelpful patterns started? Chris: "My pattern of panic attacks started straight after my disaster call. It was in my office at work and I was by myself."

B.   What stressors or changes were occurring in your life around the start of your unhelpful patterns? Chris: "Looking back, I realise I had been neglecting the client. I had been avoiding them for some time before the negotiation because if I am being honest, I was slightly intimated by them."

C. How often do your unhelpful patterns occur and how long do they last? Chris: "A panic attack can last about 10 or 15 minutes, but the effects never really go away. I feel anxious and on the verge of panic all of the time. I have been avoiding my client for about three months."

D. What significant persons or patterns are absent when your unhelpful patterns occur? Chris: "It happens mainly when I think about or talk to clients at work. Sometimes panic occurs when I am by myself in the car on the way to work."

E. Where do your unhelpful patterns occur? Chris: "At work, especially in my office. They can also happen at home usually on a Sunday evening as I know I have work the next day."

F. What are the steps involved in the generation of your unhelpful pattern? Put another way, can you identify the stages where you go from not doing unhelpful patterns to doing them? Chris: "That's easy. Whenever I think about a client and when I have to call one. Just looking at my diary, or a reminder on my phone can trigger panic. When I feel panic, I take myself off to sit in a toilet cubicle. Then I have to force myself into my office and call a client. By then I am a wreck. Clients often ask me if I am ok."

G. When do your unhelpful patterns NOT occur? Chris: "That's a hard question. Sometimes I talk to my manager or a colleague prior to a client call. They think I am doing a bit of strategising, but in reality, I am just trying to stop the panic. However, a call can go better when I do this."

H. What do you think other people know about your unhelpful pattern e.g. friends, family or colleagues? Chris: "I honestly don't know. I can't bring myself to tell anyone. I think they would want to support me."

I. What are your beliefs about your unhelpful patterns? For example; I can never change it; it's my fault that I have it. Chris: "I am a failure and a coward for being intimidated by that client."

Chris now has lots of useful information with which to help him lay down new, helpful patterns. For example, he knows the relationship with his client was based on a pattern of fear and feeling intimated, which resulted in a pattern of avoidance. Using this insight, Chris can work on his confidence to lay down relationship patterns based on self-confidence and self-assuredness, resulting in a pattern of client engagement. Chris also knew that when he talked to someone prior to making a call such as his manager or a colleague, he didn't panic. Given this, Chris can lay down a new relationship pattern of seeking support when he is struggling.

Looking back at 'The Cliff Edge' table, take one of your unhelpful patterns and ask yourself these pattern questions. Like Chris, how can your answers help you lay down helpful patterns?

The strongest source of emotion

The key to laying down a new pattern is making it more emotionally persuasive than the old one. Unless and until this happens, the old one will be hard to shift. Remember: old patterns, including unhelpful ones, formed for positive reasons. Our mind/body systems will take some persuading that old patterns and the benefits they bring, should be replaced. What does persuade them is evidence: lots of concrete evidence that new patterns are more positive and beneficial. And when we find the evidence and present it, something beautiful happens: the old pattern is replaced by the new one. This is because our mind/body systems lock on to the strongest source of emotion.

Positives and benefits of old patterns	Greater positives and benefits of new patterns
Pattern 1	New pattern 1
Pattern 2	New pattern 2
Pattern 3	New pattern 3

Pattern interruption

When my eldest daughter was a baby, she would often make life difficult for her father by refusing to drink her milk. On one particular occasion, when she had refused to drink her milk for the umpteenth time at home, I changed our feeding pattern. I took her to the baby changing room of a local supermarket, where to my great relief she proceeded to drink the whole lot. While she quickly got wise to my cunning, I saw that day how effective pattern interruption could be.

Pattern interruption is the addition of a new element or elements to an unhelpful pattern in order to change and transform it into a helpful one. There are three main ways this can be done:

- By changing how unhelpful patterns are viewed
- By changing how unhelpful patterns are done or carried out
- By introducing and using resources

These three principles can be broken down into the following techniques and strategies:

- Time

  - change how often unhelpful patterns are carried out
  - do them more quickly or slowly
  - vary when they happen
  - change how long they take.

Phillip agreed to answer/reply to phone calls from his demanding mother every four days rather than on demand, which resulted in him feeling more in control of his life.

Lizzie agreed to 'speed' worry around her house, going from room to room as quickly as she could and worrying at 'top speed'. The result? She started laughing instead of worrying.

Freya's self-esteem issues meant she felt 'exposed' when holding her head up high in public, so she started going out at less busy times of the day with her head up and then proceeded to go out later and later as the day got busier and her confidence increased.

Jeff agreed to dedicate a particular time of his day to thinking about losing his wife to illness rather than allow his thoughts to occur randomly throughout the whole day.

- Space and place

  - change where unhelpful patterns takes place

- change how the space is arranged (move objects around)
- add new contents into the space

Adrian, a student, moved the scissors with which he self-harmed from his bedroom to his communal kitchen.

Beth tackled her self-esteem issues by applying make-up in a friend's room before a night out rather than in her own room where she found it too difficult.

- Order and sequence

  - vary the order of elements or stages of unhelpful patterns
  - break down patterns into smaller stages.

Teresa agreed to put on her favourite shoes when she felt the need to binge on food with the result that she didn't binge.

Marc agreed to give his car keys to a friend so that if he wanted to get hold of some drugs he had to go on a long journey via public transport. He discovered drugs were no longer that important.

Phil and Barbara were able to overcome their fear of driving by starting off on quiet roads and building up to driving on motorways by driving on all of the different road types in between

Geeta processed a difficult trauma by interspersing her re-calling of it with clips from hilarious clips from her favourite Charlie Chaplin movies.

- Positives and negatives

  - combine unhelpful patterns with unrewarding activities

·   combine helpful patterns with rewarding ones.

Jane overcame her OCD by agreeing to hop up and down on one leg 100x if she checked her college work more than an agreed number of times, and rewarded herself with a cup of green tea if she checked her work the agreed number of times.

Sarah agreed to make her four housemates breakfast in bed for a whole week if she failed to get up and go to university.

- Change the context

    ·   change how unhelpful patterns are understood
    ·   change what they mean
    ·   change the conditions.

Sharon agreed to hand over her treasured mobile phone to a friend and only got it back when she had been to the gym. Sharon's resistance to exercise became something she looked forward to.

Raj, who was in danger of failing his Masters Degree for no good reason other than laziness, told his parents that if he slipped behind again they were not to pay for his snowboarding holiday. Raj graduated.

- Change the make-up or blueprint

    ·   observe unhelpful patterns as they are being carried out
    ·   reflect and comment on them
    ·   add surprising or unexpected elements.

I once worked with a stepfather of two teenage daughters. When he came to me, their relationship had deteriorated completely with mutual hatred on both sides. He said they hated him because he was their stepfather, a reality he felt powerless to change. What I established was that a verbal request from the stepfather, for example, 'Can you do the washing-up, please?' was a main trigger of conflict. The solution? He acquired a flipchart stand and paper from work, placed it in his kitchen and wrote out his 'polite requests' and left the room. What happened surprised them all. Removing the verbal exchanges between and himself reduced the emotional temperature. His stepdaughters, left to wash-up by themselves, did so more willingly and over time their relationship improved.

The Cliff Edge revisited

Now you have reached the end of the chapter and learnt about the impact of the patterns in your life, have another go at The Cliff Edge activity. As you complete the table, ask yourself whether you will be avoiding more cliff edges and spending more time in your 'over there'.

The Wrong Date: a new relationship with unhelpful patterns

I came up with this analogy to help a client change their relationship with all of the unhelpful patterns in their life.

Imagine you are out one evening socialising with friends. Someone engages you in conversation and offers to buy you a drink. You politely decline their kind offer, making a mental note this person is definitely not your type. At the end of the evening, which included dinner with this person, you leave in a state of bafflement. "But they're not my type," you say to yourself. The evening, you reflect, was depressing. A month and several dates later, you are amazed at the amount of time you are spending with someone who offers you nothing. And yet you are. Two holidays later, plans are being made to move in with this person. Nothing has changed. They are still not your type. In fact, they really irritate you. It's a while since you last saw your friends. 5 years pass, an engagement party and a date for your wedding...

...this would never happen to you, would it?

Patterns	Cliff Edges	Over There
Where you focus your attention	e.g. I will avoid this Cliff Edge by...	e.g. I will take myself over there by...
How you think and what you think of		
How you remember your memories/past		
Your beliefs about yourself, others and the world		
How you behave; your behaviours		
How you feel; your emotions/feelings		
Your relationships – people, places, objects		
Academic/educational and professional/work		

Summary of Chapter Three

- Patterns are anything featuring regularly in our lives that can be helpful and unhelpful.
- We can be aware or unaware of our patterns. Becoming aware of them is vital if we are to replace unhelpful patterns with helpful ones.
- Use the Cliff Edge story and exercise to help you get to know your patterns.
- Pattern matching is how our brains compare new sensory information coming in through our senses to old information stored in our memory banks.
- Pattern interruption is how we 'interrupt' unhelpful patterns so we can lay down helpful ones.

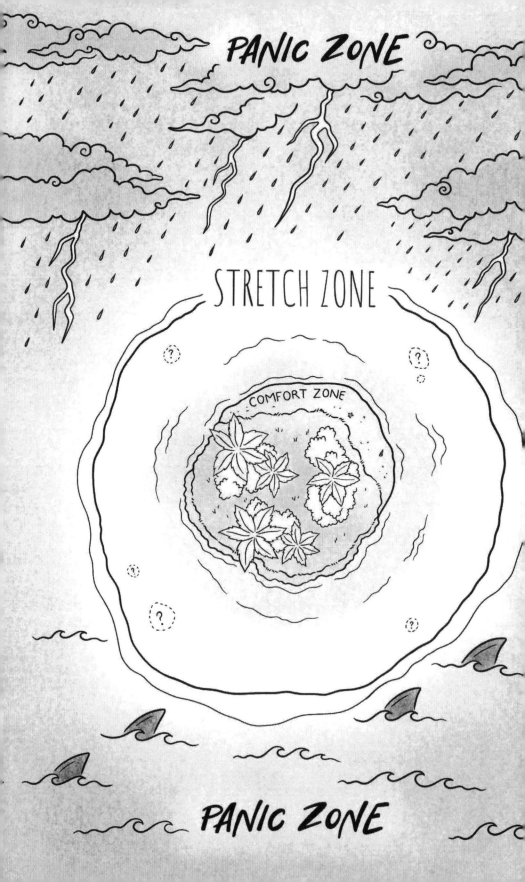

Stretch Zone

The Stretch Zone is a well-known model that enables challenge to work for you rather than against you. It is made up of three circles.

- The inner circle represents your Comfort Zone. Do be misled by the name. Your Comfort Zone is where you are trying to escape from. It is where you hide away from what scares and challenges you.
- The middle circle is called your Stretch Zone. This is a where you are trying to get to because it is a place of growth and transformation.
- The third circle is your Panic Zone. Anyone who spends all or most of their time in their Comfort Zone will know this place well because it represents what they keep stepping into when they risk leaving their Comfort Zone.

The aim is to step out of your Comfort Zone and into your Stretch Zone. Your Stretch Zone will not be an easy place to be in because it will challenge and stretch you. However, it will not be so uncomfortable that you can't get used to being there. How do you know you have stepped into your Stretch Zone? Because your first instinct will be to stay put rather than seek the security of your Comfort Zone.

What you are trying to avoid is stepping out of your Comfort Zone and straight into your Panic Zone. Panic Zones explain themselves.

Spending more and more time in your Stretch Zone will take some experimentation as you find out how to get and spend more time there. Hang in there because when you get it right, the magic starts. The more time you spend in your Stretch Zone, the bigger it gets. And the bigger it gets, the smaller the other two Zones become. Spend enough time in your Stretch Zone and it becomes both your place of rest and activity.

You may spend some time in either your Comfort or Panic Zones, but no more than anyone else.

A is for Acceptance

Many years ago, I was seeing a therapist to help me through a challenging period. In one session, my therapist sat back and made the following observation: **"You have to accept your reality. There is no choice in this."** He said this because after several sessions of therapy I was going around in circles on a particular issue. If I'm being completely honest, I found my therapist's comment irritating at the time. I was not interested in accepting my reality because at that time my 'reality' was pretty bleak. Why would I accept it?

I still see that therapist from time to time largely because they are good at what they do, but also because on that day, they understood me better than anyone else had ever done. They understood that I was afraid to accept myself for who I was, and my life for what it was. Rather than accept, I lived a fantasy existence until my therapist helped me bring it to an end. A few years later I came up with my own concept to help people as I had been helped that day. This I called my 'Fantasy-Reality Gap.'

Fantasy-Reality Gaps (FRG)

Consider the following statements:

- who you are, and who you will be
- what you are doing, and what you will be doing
- how your life is, and how your life will be

Understood in this way, FRGs are simply the difference between our current and future realities. We all have them because we all live in the present and we all move towards the future. From this perspective, FRGs are something we all have in common.

When FRGs become helpful or unhelpful, is when I become interested as a mental health practitioner. This is explained by the subjects of this chapter: acceptance and non-acceptance. As we shall see, acceptance results in helpful FRGs that enable us to make progress in life. Whereas non-acceptance results in unhelpful FRGs that exhaust us in the pursuit of the impossible, or on the contrary, exhaust us because we don't pursue anything at all.

My aim in this chapter is for my FRG concept to:

- explain difficulties and challenges in terms of acceptance and non-acceptance
- explain your own difficulties and challenges in these terms
- help you overcome non-acceptance and to achieve acceptance.

The FRG Spectrum: acceptance to non-acceptance

"I went to see Mark at a time when my eating habits were out of control. I had been a serial yo-yo dieter for years and had gone back and forth to various popular dieting clubs but always ended up putting any weight I had lost back on. I realised that there must be a reason why I felt the need to eat excessively, sometimes in secret, at times and longed to establish a normal relationship with food which I could sustain for life.

Going back to a conversation we had in our first meeting Mark raised a point that sometimes people have a 'fantasy' about the person they are or want to be and I recall at the time that I did feel a little aggrieved by that comment but I actually think he hit the nail on the head. I have given this concept a lot of thought since then and have come to realise that there is a part of me who enjoys the idea of doing certain things more than the actual execution of it and actually, it is that part of me that sets the unrealistic and unachievable goals which then has a knock on effect with my poor eating habits and leads me to be unhappy and so the cycle continues. I am now learning to do what I actually enjoy doing, when I am able to do it and will focus on that for the time being. I am feeling very positive about the future and a lot more content with myself..." Emma

My FRGs break down into the following three areas: who we are, what we do and the lives we lead. At one end of the spectrum lies acceptance, which results in helpful FRGs. These can be captured by the statements below:

- who I am, is who I think I am
- who I am, is who I want to be

- who I want to be, is who I can be

- what I am doing, is what I think I am doing
- what I am doing, is what I want to be doing
- what I want to do, is what I can do

- how my life is, how I think my life is
- how my life is, is how I want my life to be
- how I want my life to be, is how my life can be.

At the other end of the spectrum is non-acceptance, which results in unhelpful FRGs. These can be captured by these statements:

- who I am, is not who I think I am
- who I am, is not who I think I should be
- who I want to be, is not who I can be

- what I am doing, is not what I think I am doing
- what I am doing, is not what I think I should be doing
- what I want to do, is not what I can do

- how my life is, is not what I think it is
- how my life is, is not how I think it should be
- how I want my life to be, is not how it can be.

Activity

Taking each of the above statements, consider which of them apply to you. Write down all of the statements you feel do apply. If you are unsure, make a best guess. When a friend of mine did this exercise, she said it took her two full days of reflection because it made her 'reappraise my entire life.' Now, I am not suggesting you take two days, but I am encouraging you to take some time because the topic is so important.

What did you discover about how accepting or non-accepting you are? About whether FRGs play a helpful or unhelpful role in your life? How many of the different statements types did you list? Which of the areas do they relate to – who you are, what you do and the life you lead? Keep your list, thoughts and reflections, so you can revisit them throughout the chapter.

How can I tell if my FRGs are helpful or unhelpful?

"I spent years thinking I was someone who could form a certain type of relationship, a fantasy that years of disappointment and evidence to the contrary failed to dislodge. The FRG was a revelation not only because it opened my eyes to this fact, but it also explained why I had been so angry and destructive for so long. How do I know this? Because my anger disappeared overnight when I accepted that who I was, was who I wanted to be." Francesca

In simple terms, if we are making progress in life, if our difficulties are overcome and our challenges achieved, there is a good chance our FRGs are helpful and we are living lives of acceptance. If the opposite is true, if our difficulties and challenges persist, then there is a good chance our FRGs are unhelpful and we are struggling with acceptance.

Helpful or unhelpful FRGs tend to go hand-in-hand with certain types of thinking, behaving, feeling and relationships. In the table overpage are examples that go with both. With your statements from the previous activity in mind, look down the list to consider which if any you relate to.

Signs of an unhelpful FRG	Signs of a helpful FRG
Poor mental health and wellbeing:	**Good mental health and well-being:**
difficult emotions such as stress, anxiety, depression or anger	positive emotions such as joy, gratitude, interest or serenity
self-criticism/negative self-talk	self-appreciation/positive self-talk
negative thoughts, unwanted intrusive thoughts	positive thoughts, clear mind
negative, self-limiting beliefs	positive, self-empowering beliefs
low self-esteem, self-worth and low confidence	good level of self-esteem/worth/confidence
negative memories	positive memories
tiredness, fatigue, exhaustion	high energy levels, quick recovery, resilient
poor motivation	good levels of motivation
poor sleep	good sleep
Negative behaviours:	**Positive behaviours:**
avoidance	engagement
procrastination	productivity
perfectionism	good enough, stretched and challenged
fear of failure	good risk taking, setbacks are opportunities
impatience, frustration	patience, contentedness
obsessive, compulsive, addictive	restrained, controlled, self-possessed
self-sabotage, destructive	self-supporting, building
denial, secrecy	openness, honesty, transparency
poor self-care/neglect	good self-care

Signs of an unhelpful FRG	Signs of a helpful FRG
Relationships:	**Relationships:**
criticism, judgment	support, respect
concern	relaxed
gameplaying	normal relationships
blurred boundaries	clear boundaries
unconfident, people pleasing	assertive
comparisons with others, jealousy/envy	I'm ok, you're ok
dismissal and intolerance of others	acceptance and tolerance of others
arrogance/self-promotion	humility
withdrawn, avoidant	connected
argumentative	agreeable
irritability	enjoyment
blaming, others are responsible	approving, taking responsibility
Unhelpful change strategies:	**Helpful change strategies:**
unrealistic expectations	realistic expectations
quick fix	commitment to what it takes
reject support	seek support
inflexibility – Plan A must work	flexibility – happy to switch to a Plan B

What did you discover?

Can you see a relationship between your FRG statements and your signs? Which of the following statements best describe what you found?

- Acceptance is not an issue for me.
- Acceptance might be an issue for me.
- Acceptance is an issue for me.

Taking a closer look

If you discovered your FRGs are helpful and you don't have difficulties with acceptance, then it maybe your difficulties and challenges have nothing to do with acceptance. In this case the other stages of my IMPACT may be more relevant for you. However, if you discovered acceptance is an issue and you need to gain a better understanding of your unhelpful FRGs, below are some areas to consider where yours might exist. Note down the areas you feel could be relevant.

> "I liked to take drugs. It was my reward and my escape. There were downsides, but I pushed or tried to push those away. My fantasy was that I could be happy in myself, a good husband and father, a successful businessman and still smoke. The hard truth was that I couldn't and wasn't."

Yourself

- identity
- status
- beliefs
- self-esteem and self-worth
- personal qualities and characteristics

- physical appearance
- intelligence
- capabilities
- sexuality, gender
- abilities, strengths and weaknesses.

Your personal and professional circumstances

- social and cultural circumstances
- environment
- relationship status
- wealth
- professional status
- employment
- past, present and future.

Your resources – internal and external

- psychological abilities: resilience, flexibility, emotional regulation
- positive mental health and wellbeing
- money
- time
- information and knowledge
- skills and abilities
- people.

Your goals

- personal
- collective i.e. involve one or more people
- academic
- professional.

Your strategies for achieving change

- goal setting
- planning and preparation
- mindset.

What did you discover?

Were you surprised or did it confirm what you already knew? For some having a better understanding of their FRGs and the issue of acceptance can be greatly relieving, while for others it can be distressing. Whatever your response, remember, acceptance is not a choice, but a necessity. At some point unhelpful FRGs have to be closed if poor mental health and emotional wellbeing is to be avoided.

Prioritising your FRGs

If acceptance is or might be an issue, then this is what I will ask you to do next. Going back to the areas you noted down, the next stage is to consider which are the most problematic for you. If we don't have a good understanding of our priority areas, we run the risk of focusing on areas which are less important or worse of no importance at all. Misdiagnosis of any problem can only make it worse. Using a 0 to 10 scale, where 0 means there is no problem at all and 10 means the opposite, choose a number that reflects the importance of each of your areas. Anything scored 7 or above can be considered a priority area. Anything scored 5 or 6 can be considered a lesser priority. And anything scored 4 or below can be left or even ignored. Now you know your priority areas, the better placed you are to work through and overcome them, and in the process close your FRGs through acceptance.

Measuring your FRG: the 0-10 scale

Taking the priority areas you have identified, now choose a number that represents where your unhelpful FRG is now, followed by a second number that represents where you would like it to be i.e. when it has become a helpful FRG. Thinking about your second number and looking back at the signs of a helpful FRG in the table on Pages 81 & 82:

- what is different about you?
- what are you doing differently?
- how is your life different?

What is it like to live with an unhelpful FRG?

I once worked with Damian, a university student. In our first session, Damian told me he was far behind with his studies due to a combination of "laziness" and "smoking far too much marijuana." When Damian woke up for his lectures, he thought, oh sod it and went back to sleep. Damian was highly critical of himself and wanted me to help him "get a grip." The reality was rather different. Therapy helped Damian to realise he was actually severely depressed and had been for most of his life since severe bullying at primary and secondary school. Once Damian accepted his 'laziness' and marijuana addiction was actually an unhelpful FRG he was able to make progress.

If you are not who you think you are, if you are not doing what you think you are doing, and if how your life is, is not what you think it is, then as Damian found, life can be difficult and challenging. An unhelpful FRG threatens our ability to thrive and survive, and while it remains unhelpful, our Emotional Self, who we have met now on many occasions, will let us know through sending appropriate 'emotional' messages.

Why do FRGs become unhelpful?

No one sets out to live life undermined by an unhelpful FRG. As I said at the start of the chapter, we all have an FRG, it's just that for very human reasons it can become unhelpful. Maybe someone didn't know they had one because they never learnt or were told about it. Or maybe they did know, it's just that they lost sight of it in the busyness of their lives. Or maybe the personal significance of someone's dreams and ambitions, their achievement or failure, meant they overrode the warning signs when their FRG became unhelpful. Whatever the reason, the fantasy self, behaviours and life are accepted as true. This makes it easy for a vicious cycle to establish itself. The FRG continues to grow because someone doesn't know it exists. And how can something that doesn't exist be addressed? This was exactly what happened to me.

Types of unhelpful FRG

Confidence

Someone with an unconfident FRG will underestimate themselves and what they are capable of. They will downplay the impact of what they do and will live a life of unrealised potential. An unconfident FRG makes disappointment and failures the norm. Any positives will be put down to external factors such as luck and the sympathy of others and NOT down to the efforts of the person themselves. Indeed positives can feel so difficult and uncomfortable to someone with an unconfident FRG that they are actively avoided. Conversely, someone with an over-confident FRG will overestimate themselves and what they are capable of. They will overplay the impact of what they do and just like their underconfident counterpart will live a life of unrealised potential. An over-confident FRG leads someone to assume success is inevitable and mistake failure for accomplishment. Other people will be responsible for failures, and successes will be solely down to the individual. Setbacks and disappointments will feel as unpleasant to them as achievements do to someone with an unconfident FRG.

Stages of life

Tom was a newly qualified doctor when he first came to me for support. Not only was he struggling to cope professionally, he had also lost his ability to function generally. He wasn't eating well, his new one-bedroom flat was empty but for a few necessary pieces of furniture, and his kitchen full of unused appliances. Tom had also become socially withdrawn from his family, partner and friends. What emerged for Tom in his therapy was that he had never struggled in life. "I came from a wealthy family. I went to a top public school. I was bright. I had friends. I moved seamlessly through my education and into work. I have never known a time when who I was, was not enough. I have always been able to expand my capacity to cope and deal with life, until now. Who I thought I was is not who I now am. I thought I was my all-conquering-self fighting a battle I didn't know I was losing."

Stages of life FRGs can affect anyone at any stage of life. They can be evident from an early age or like Tom emerge much later in life. A Stages of Life FRG that becomes too large is when someone moves into a new life stage without adapting to it. In Tom's case, he lacked the self-awareness to adapt, and continued to live as the person he was previously.

Stages of Life FRGs I come across are:

- school/educational transitions
- education into employment
- career change/transition
- relationship stages and changes
- moving to a new house/area

General and specific

General

One Stage of Life FRG that swept my legs from under me a few years ago was the assumption that my life would unfold in a general way. I assumed financial and material wealth, professional status and the ability to provide a certain lifestyle for my children would all just fall into place. This fantasy trajectory my life was supposed to take belonged to my father. Although I knew this at some level, what I lost sight of was that my life path had always been very different from his. It was a house move that brought me crashing down. Not only did I not have my father's wealth, the house-move revealed I didn't have any wealth at all. Although the period of depression that followed appeared to come out of nowhere, the truth was it had been building for some time. It's just that the life I thought I was leading turned out to be a fantasy.

Specific

General FRGs like mine are based on assumptions that life will provide in some vague, ill-defined way. Specific FRGs are when someone has a clear idea of what they are working towards, be that a desired lifestyle or a specific life goal, it's just that the lifestyle or goal were either unrealistic in the first place, or if they weren't, the person's strategies to achieve them were.

Other people & FRGs

Some unhelpful FRGs are connected to people we are close to. Families—parents, siblings & extended family— can deliberately or unintentionally set children along a fantasy path in life that reflects their values and beliefs rather than the child's. If this is done with good, if misplaced intentions, then the child might willingly set off down the path given to them. However, if the intentions are less positive, they might do so out of fear. Children often do as they are told because they don't know any better, and because they have a keen sense of what they stand to lose or gain. Disapproval and rejection, acceptance and validation, often live at the heart of unhelpful FRGs that 'belong' to families.

Family values and beliefs can also result in the overestimation or underestimation of children and their abilities. I once worked with a young man in his early 20s, whose low self-esteem and self-worth resulted in serial underachievement. I will never forget what he said to me in our very first session. He said even at primary school, he knew he would be the one who would not go to university. The explanation? As early as he could remember, his father had belittled him on a daily basis. This type of unhelpful FRG often goes hand-in-hand with the Confidence FRG.

Other FRGs connected to people we know well, do not originate with them but are intended to benefit or impact on them in some way. For example, when someone is motivated to improve the quality of someone's life, making them proud, or when they are seeking to prove someone wrong, making them jealous. In such cases, the recipient may or may not be aware of the person's intentions.

Sometimes people are motivated to become like someone else

because we find them and the lives, they lead, inspirational in some way. These can be people known or unknown to us – such as celebrities.

A means of escape

Self-esteem is in my experience a significant factor in creating unhelpful FRGs. Someone with low self-esteem is often someone who doesn't like who they are or how their lives are unfolding. Unhelpful FRGs can be an understandable response to this. A fantasy self and life are created as a means of escape because acceptance can be too painful. Too much self-esteem can also be an issue. FRGs open up because someone believes themselves to be more capable or successful than they really are.

Unhelpful FRGs can be a response to adversity such as trauma or loss, when in an understandable desire to improve their life circumstances and chances, someone loses sight of how they can realistically change both themselves and their lives. There can often be a great deal of shame or regret attached to trauma and loss, which can also result in an unhelpful FRG.

Barriers to acceptance

Some people find acceptance easy to achieve and live their lives with helpful FRGs, while for others it is less easy. Overpage are some barriers to acceptance that I come across most often in my work.

A lack of awareness

If we don't know something exists, how can we do anything about it? Unfortunately, unhelpful FRGs do not announce themselves with a neon sign. There are no texts, emails or DMs informing us of their presence. On page 95 I look at triggers of awareness, but until they occur, we can be left in a state of ignorance. Emotions like depression and anxiety, unrealistic expectations and difficult relationships can all negatively affect our awareness. Luckily for most people being unconscious of their unhelpful FRGs, is a temporary state of affairs. This is because lacking conscious awareness of an unhelpful FRG at the level of thought and imagination, rarely equates to no conscious awareness at all. Have another look at the signs of unhelpful FRGs on pages 81 & 82. All of them are potential sources of awareness, which indicate that something is not quite right in our lives. In the end, signs like these become so problematic they provoke us into doing something about them – like talking to someone like me or picking up a book like this.

Plan A isn't working, but Plan B is too much work

Awareness gives us the psychological flexibility to keep an eye on our FRGs and to keep them helpful. When they are helpful, who we are, what we do and how we live our lives—otherwise known as Plan A—can stay as it is. Plan A's are great, but they come with an Achilles Heel: they are often the result of a lot of blood, sweat and tears. When we change or the world changes around us necessitating a Plan B, the sheer enormity of the effort required to develop it can often prove too much. Defeated, we fall back into the warm embrace of Plan A, which takes no effort at all. When this happens our FRG has become unhelpful because we are now running and organising our lives using a plan that has stopped working. Our only option is to accept that we need a Plan B and sometimes we can't accept this.

Letting go

Transforming an FRG from unhelpful to helpful, while necessary, can be hard because it involves letting go of who we have been, what we have been doing and the life we were leading. Even though these three areas of our lives were causing our difficulties and challenges, for a long time we imagined they represented a resolution. Accepting that we might have been mistaken in some or all of these aspects, can be hard.

Adrian, a young man in his 20s who I worked with, was testament to how hard letting go can be. When he first came to see me, he was severely depressed, actively suicidal and self-harming. Although we had made some initial progress, by our fourth session he had relapsed. In seeking to make sense of his relapse, Adrian realised the following. He was terrified of no longer being depressed. To him, being happy, was an alien notion. Therapy was offering him a glimpse of who he could be, and this shook him badly. Adrian thought his depressed self was who he was. He thought his depressed life was his life. 'I thought I knew who I was. My fear was that I might glimpse happiness but fail to sustain it, and that terrifies me more than staying depressed.' Adrian found acceptance and transformed his unhelpful FRG into a helpful one because therapy showed him a safe way to do so.

The benefits of acceptance

As Damian, Tom and Adrian discovered, acceptance does not mean giving up on overcoming difficulties or achieving challenges. Acceptance is not resignation, but a stage of transformation. If this were not true, why are there so many benefits to acceptance, such as increased energy, better mental health, improved relationships and increased confidence? Perhaps the biggest benefit though is how acceptance can reveal the capabilities and potential someone possesses, which were hidden by their unhelpful FRG. And while these capabilities and potentials may be more or less than they imagined because they are a true reflection, they result in an FRG that helps rather than hinders. Someone who has not found acceptance and who has an unhelpful FRG is likely to mistake the benefits of acceptance as belonging to their fantasy self and life. However, only genuine acceptance results in genuine benefits.

A virtuous circle

A significant amount of negative emotion felt by someone will only exist because their FRG is unhelpful. Closing it through acceptance, therefore, switches that amount off. Herein lies the beauty of the FRG idea. Closing an unhelpful FRG redirects the energy used in the generation of negative emotions into the generation of positive ones. With more positive emotion and increased energy levels, the conflict between our 'Rational and Emotional Selves' that often characterises unhelpful FRGs, is replaced with cooperation. Possibilities previously dismissed or rejected can now be considered and acted upon as we feel motivated to turn good ideas into real ones.

Closing our FRGs through acceptance, because it contributes to our thriving and surviving, is music to the ears of our Emotional Self which communicates its happiness with us through positive emotional messages.

Finding acceptance

Unhelpful FRGs make life miserable. Most people therefore are nudged, pushed or elbowed into finding acceptance because of the overwhelming need to do so. Yes, finding acceptance requires an increase in self-awareness, but once it has been achieved finding acceptance can be hard to resist. People do resist, at least initially like Adrian, but because they gain a glimpse of what life can be like, so finding it becomes too persuasive.

Until my therapist got me to this stage, I was going nowhere. Until Damian, Tom and Adrian got to this stage, they were going nowhere either. The good thing about self-awareness is the wide-range of factors that can trigger it. The trick of course is recognising the triggers for what they are. For most of us at least one of the factors below intervenes to increase our awareness that we are living life with an unhelpful FRG:

A self-help book!	Boredom
Life becomes harder than it needs to be	Consequences
We come to really dislike or even hate ourselves	Responsibility
Time	A memory
An event or incident	A Conversation with Impact had by accident or design
Maturity	A glimpse of the benefits of change
	Inspiration

What is it like to live life with a helpful FRG?

If who you are, is who you think you are, if what you are doing, is what you think you are doing, and if how your life is, is how you think your life is, then you are boosting your ability to thrive and survive. Look back to pages 81 & 82 and the signs of a helpful FRG. This is how life can be. A helpful FRG means you make hay while the sun shines, but no longer fear when it stops. Look at what happened to the stories of Damian, Tom and Adrian. Damian graduated and is now pursuing a career in journalism. Tom settled into his medical career. And Adrian finished his engineering apprenticeship. Finding acceptance and a helpful FRG enabled all three to move on to and ultimately through the next two stages of the IMPACT model.

Summary of Chapter Four:

- Fantasy-Reality Gaps capture the difference between what we think our current reality is and what it actually is. The bigger the FRG, the more problematic it is.
- Closing unhelpful FRGs is essential for positive mental health and wellbeing.
- Acceptance of our current reality is how we change our FRGs from unhelpful to helpful.
- There are different types of FRG and different causes of them.
- Finding acceptance can be difficult, but achieving it comes with clear benefits.

ADDICTION **BURNOUT** DEPRESSION
CRISIS

NO FLEXIBILITY
NO AWARENESS

SIGNS & CLUES
MISSED OR IGNORED

ONE VISIT ONLY

THE LINE WHERE ALL THINGS ARE POSSIBLE

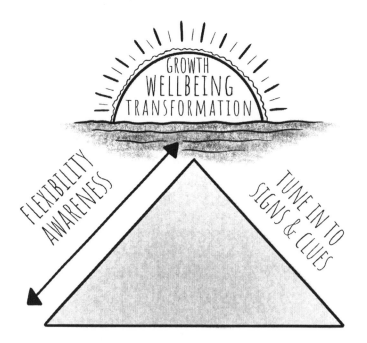

GROWTH
WELLBEING
TRANSFORMATION

FLEXIBILITY
AWARENESS

TUNE IN TO
SIGNS & CLUES

REFLECT, ADAPT, LEARNING

THE LINE WHERE ALL THINGS ARE POSSIBLE

The Triangle of Possibility

Along the bottom side of the triangle is the Line Where All Things Are Possible. Within the natural laws of the universe, any and every solution to your difficulties and challenges exists along this line. The aim is to move upwards along the sides of the triangle until you get to the Point Where Only One Thing Is Possible. When you reach the PWOOTIP, you should be exactly where you want and need to be.

As human beings we have no choice but to move forwards in time and space, which means that we have to move from a potentially infinite set of choices to a single one. This is the decision-making process. Whenever you make a decision, big or small, you will have travelled from the LWATAP to the PWOOTIP. The goal is to be in control of your journey between the two.

Stress, anxiety and depression; addictions, compulsions and obsessions – all represent a loss of control of our journey to the PWOOTIP. Burnout, panic attacks, suicidal thoughts/actions and personal destruction all represent PWOOTIP where we have lost control.

Self-awareness and psychological flexibility are how we can avoid ending up at harmful PWOOTIP. As we set off from the LWATAP and head towards the PWOOTIP, self-awareness allows us to tune in to the emotions generated on our journey. Psychological flexibility allows us to make decisions based on those emotions.

The good news is we have an ally on our journey – our Emotional Self. It journeys ahead of us to the likely PWOOTIP of our current journey. If it likes what it sees, it will let us know through the message of positive emotions. If it doesn't like what it sees, the message will be very different.

Using our self-awareness, we can tune into those emotions and understand what our Emotional Self is trying to tell us. We can then use our psychological flexibility to decide whether to continue – or not.

With difficult emotions, our Emotional Self is telling us to turn around and head back towards our LWATAP, so we can regroup before heading off on a new journey. The goal is for each new journey to last longer than the one before as we apply what we have learnt. If they aren't longer or if we never actually reach a positive PWOOTIP then we know something needs to change. What needs to change will be located somewhere within my IMPACT model.

And if, despite our Emotional Self warning us to turn around, we still end up at a harmful PWOOTIP, then we are not in a good place.

C is for Challenge

There isn't a living thing on the planet that isn't engaged in making the best of being alive. Being alive is a challenge, and to do it well human beings need to both thrive and survive. Fairly or unfairly, evolution has determined that achieving the optimum state of thriving and surviving requires continual investment. Challenge is not therefore a choice, and this is why it is a stage in the IMPACT model.

There are plenty of ways in which human beings represent the nature of challenge, and what challenge means to us. In my work, I am continuously amazed by the sources my clients are inspired by:

- themselves
- significant people in their lives
- celebrities
- stories, literature, poetry
- film, theatre, television
- philosophy

- the news
- social media
- education, academia
- professions and careers.

The good news is that the human race possesses the innate determination to help us rise to the challenge. We know how to thrive and survive in almost any circumstances. The challenge is to make that knowledge work for us.

> "The film 'The Shawshank Redemption' cropped up a lot talking to Mark. The final scenes when Tim Robbins is crawling through the sewer, knowing that at the end was his boat on the beach, was one we talked about as being symbolic of my relationship with challenge. The film really helped me befriend challenge when until then it had been my enemy." Tony

The nature of challenge

Challenge is good (most of the time)

Challenge is undoubtedly a good thing when it enables us to achieve personal, academic and professional growth. In good times challenge results in a sense of achievement, pride and satisfaction and in difficult times, it builds resilience and helps us to feel secure. A challenge met, helps us to get through difficult times more easily.

When challenge is less positive is when it exists in a form that prevents someone from progressing in life through no fault of their own, no matter how committed they are to overcoming it. In writing this book and this chapter, I am acutely aware that many people find themselves in the position where challenge will never be a positive force in their life. Since 2005 I have worked to support individuals to overcome some of the most severe challenges anyone can face, but when I have been unsuccessful it has sometimes been because my clients and I were up against a form of challenge that does not respect an individual's desire to realise their potential. So, sadly, my IMPACT model and this book is not for that form of challenge. Everything I write below therefore assumes that someone—maybe you—can overcome their challenges and achieve their Transformation even in the most difficult of circumstances.

Evolving challenge

Challenge is a constant in our lives, but how it presents itself will evolve as we go through the different stages of our lives. It can be predictable and unpredictable, announced and unannounced, short-lived and lifelong, mental and physical. What most people know is that the one constant of challenge is it is never the same.

Challenging language

When you describe who you are to yourself or to others, what do we you have to say on the subject of challenge? What language do you use? As you begin this chapter, try to capture your relationship with challenge through language. For example, do you 'avoid' or 'embrace' challenge, 'welcome' or 'fear' it? Is challenge connected to your 'past', 'present' or 'future'? If you were being interviewed for a job, for example, and you were asked about how you cope with challenge, how would you answer?

In the box overpage, record your language of challenge and reflect on the extent to which you use one or both columns. You can use single words or short phrases, and if your words generate images or recall memories, be more descriptive.

Self-doubt	Self-belief
List examples of typical language	List examples of typical language

The emotions of challenge

These can be both positive and helpful or negative and unhelpful depending on the person and the context. Challenge can instil feelings of fear or excitement, dread or motivation, uncertainty or relief. When we feel challenged our emotions are communicating something important about the nature of the challenge we face. In effect they are an assessment of what we face, a series of questions such as:

- have you ever been here before?
- have you been here before and failed?
- if you failed before, has anything changed since then?
- have you been here before and succeeded?
- if you succeeded, is your approach still the right one or does it need updating?
- have you established a realistic level of challenge?
- is the strategy to meet your challenge realistic?

In Chapter Two: Meaning, I introduced you to the idea of emotions as messages and how your Emotional Self uses emotions to communicate with you. When we feel difficult emotions such as fear, dread or apprehension it is important to understand what they are communicating. They are NOT saying don't bother. Rather, they are saying please be kind to yourself and go back to the drawing board. In my experience, too many people give up because of the emotions they experience, when what is required is not a change of challenge, but a change of approach. This is what this chapter is all about.

Your emotions of challenge	
List of positive emotions	List of negative emotions

A history of challenge

When the next challenge comes along, our Emotional Self will use the evidence we have given it throughout our life to help it determine which message to send. It will look back at our history of challenge. Our Emotional Self will consider what challenge means to us and how we have coped with it in its variety of forms. Are we ready? Are we prepared? Do we accept it as a part of life? Are we flexible in our response to different types of challenge? When we have a positive history with challenge, our Emotional Self generates positive, helpful emotions when the next one comes along. We go into it emotionally equipped, which has the effect of lessening the challenge as it arrives. Conversely, when we have a problematic history with challenge, our Emotional Self generates negative, unhelpful emotions when it lands on our doorstep. We go into a period of challenge emotionally ill-equipped, which amplifies the level of challenge as it begins.

Over time we establish a baseline for challenge. Each new challenge is assessed by our Emotional Self as being either below, on or above our baseline, i.e. within, on the limit of or over our ability to deal with it. Knowing our baseline is crucial especially if forgetting it results in us underestimating ourselves. Many of us are great at embracing and coping with challenge, the trick is to remember we are! An obvious point maybe, but time and again people I work with do not. Those that don't remember, typically have low self-esteem and self-worth; achievement, pride and satisfaction—because they challenge the negative view someone has of themselves—can be uncomfortable or even painful to accept. Forgetting resolves this conflict by hiding any successes where they won't be found or deleting them entirely.

"Every time I said the next challenge was too great, I reconnected with my baseline and history of challenge. It was undeniable that I DID challenge, and yet each time I would forget. I was trapped in my house by anxiety. A year later I graduated as a pharmacist. I changed my relationship with challenge and that made the difference." David

In my experience, a positive history of challenge is where someone can: "Make hay when the sun shines, have a plan for when it stops."

A lesson in challenge: riding a bike

In my work, clients often feel overwhelmed or defeated by the scale of the challenge they face. In such moments, I ask them whether they can ride a bike. Luckily, most can or remember learning. "What happened when the stabilisers came off and for the first time?" I ask.

The common response is, "I wobbled and zigzagged for a few metres, then I fell off, resulting in grazed knees and bloody elbows."

In that moment of tears and frustration, did they decide: "This whole biking thing isn't for me"? No, of course, not. Rather than being overwhelmed or defeated by the challenge, falling off simply made them more determined. The trouble with adults is they can forget their history with challenge. The failed New Year's Resolution is the equivalent to a child falling off a bike once or twice and never getting back on again.

Entry points

When we first imagine or become aware of a challenge, it can 'challenge' us in a number of ways. The following are common responses. See if you recognise any of the following:

- it feels too big or difficult to you
- you talk yourself out of it because you assume you will fail
- you can't risk the time or the money
- its future status makes it too hard for you to visualise
- other people tell you it is impossible and you believe them.

In order to get beyond these apparent 'truths', how we respond is key. One way is to discover what I call your 'entry point' which is simply the point at which progress can start to be made. To find your entry point, firstly assess how you initially feel and behave when faced with your challenge. If you feel unhelpfully stressed or anxious, or if you procrastinate, this might well be evidence that your starting point is problematic like those of the above. Difficult emotions and problematic behaviours at this point are VERY USEFUL pieces of feedback. They DO NOT mean the challenge is wrong or beyond you, rather they indicate that a new entry point is needed.

- If your challenge feels too big or difficult, break it down into smaller ones.
- Remember to hand back any thoughts of failure to the person they belong to: your Negative Self (Chapter Two: Meaning).
- Consider that finding the time and the money are really ways of backing and believing in yourself.
- If you can't visualise how your challenge will happen, change your perspective. No challenge would ever be achieved if it were necessary to see the end before the beginning.

- If other people don't believe in you, find yourself someone to give you a Conversation With Impact.

"I had lived in Spain for eight years but never learnt to speak Spanish. The fear of failure was so intense. My wife was Spanish but my fear just made us fall out whenever she tried to teach me, so we gave up. Mark suggested his entry point idea and bingo. I downloaded a language app, and then found myself an online tutor in England! and then negotiated lessons with my wife. Looking back the challenge felt too enormous, when in reality it wasn't. I will never forget the day I bought a bus ticket and ordered a meal in Spanish. I didn't fail and no one laughed at me." Lee

The challenge paradox

My entry point idea is connected to what I call the Challenge Paradox. As a practitioner, I work on the principle that if someone was able to overcome their difficulties and challenges by themselves, they would do so. If they are unable to, then this means they are currently living a life that is too challenging. This places someone in a double-bind, rendering them unable to progress while recognising that progress is necessary. This predicament I call the 'Challenge Paradox.' It is important that when someone feels unable to move forwards—when they are faced with the 'Challenge Paradox'—they are shown that this is NOT because they can't, but because they have yet to make the concept of challenge work for them. If my challenge paradox resonates with you, then my '0 to 10' Challenge exercise at the end of this chapter will show you how to escape it by finding your entry point.

The challenge of good ideas

Our Emotional Selves love a good idea, one that suggests a resolution to our difficulties and challenges. When we come up with a good idea, our Emotional Selves look kindly upon us and allow us to enjoy a honeymoon period. Instead of fear and despondency, our Emotional Selves switch to states of curiosity and anticipation, when after a period of demoralisation, the possibility of change is in the air. In the immediate aftermath of our new idea, our Emotional Selves look for a ripple effect of change triggered by its arrival. However, there is a harsh reality to new ideas. If our Emotional Selves conclude that our idea is just that—an idea—it responds in the only way it knows how: they send us messages in the form of unhelpful, difficult emotions. If our Emotional Selves could talk, we would hear them ask: "What are you playing at?" "What happened to your good idea?" but they can't talk, so they make us emotional instead. "What are you playing at?" is a negative emotion translated into words.

The Goldilocks Principle: helpful and unhelpful levels of challenge

A helpful level of challenge is one where progress is made despite the degree of difficulty a challenge represents. Establishing an optimum level of challenge is not an exact science, but a process of trial and error. Most of us make progress in a 'higgledy-piggledy' fashion, insofar as that we have good days and not so good days. The main determinant is that despite any setbacks, we are making overall progress. If we are making progress, then the level of challenge is helpful. However, if our progress comes to a halt, then the level of challenge has either become too high or has dropped too low. The Goldilocks Principle is a great way of establishing a helpful level of challenge: not too little, not too much, but just the right amount.

Challenge: the right goal, but the wrong strategy

Many people find it easy to identify the right goal to challenge themselves with, such as to lose weight or change job, but find achieving it more difficult. One explanation can be a disconnect between goal and strategy. As a client said to me once:

> "I was aiming for a summit sat on top of a different mountain to the one I was climbing."

A failure to achieve a goal is misinterpreted as evidence it is beyond someone i.e. it is too challenging. The 'right goal, but the wrong strategy,' suggests otherwise. Instead, the goal is seen as realistic and the focus shifts to changing the strategy so that it aligns with the goal i.e. 'the right goal with the right strategy'.

Types of challenge

How you tackle your challenges will be influenced by the type of challenges they represent. For example, are they challenges that only you are facing, or do they involve other people? Are your challenges of your own making or can responsibility be laid at someone else's door? Over the next few pages, I look at different types of challenges to help you better understand your own. Understanding your challenges allows you to focus your resources more accurately on overcoming them, saving you precious time and energy.

Internal and external challenges

Common internal challenges can be:

- poor mental and/or physical health
- poor overall wellbeing
- negative thinking styles/negative mindset
- negative, self-limiting beliefs
- unhelpful, self-sabotaging behaviours
- difficult emotions
- poor sense of identity or self
- low self-esteem, belief and confidence
- distressing or traumatic memories and past experiences

Common external challenges can be:

- people and relationships
- physical appeerence
- a lack of information and knowledge, or the wrong type
- ineffective strategies or approaches to problem solving
- a lack of resources or the wrong ones
- environmental factors
- organisational factors
- social and cultural factors
- gender, ethnicity, sexuality
- time and/or money

The two forms of challenge can and often do influence the other, of course. For example, when an employee experiences mental health issues (internal) due to bullying at work (external). Or when an increase in self-esteem (internal) results in positive changes to someone's relationships (external).

> "It reached the stage where I could not be alone because I was too anxious. I saw a hypnotherapist because I thought the challenge was my work, specifically my fear of public speaking. Deal with that, I thought, and my anxiety would go away. In hypnotherapy I was like Barack Obama, but when it came to actual meetings at work I fell apart. It was only when I realised the challenge was my non-existent self-esteem and not meetings at work that I began to make progress."
> Patricia

Misdiagnosing these challenges like Patricia did e.g. focusing externally when the challenge is internal, is easily done. 'Yo-yo dieting' is another good example of when the wrong type of challenge is frequently identified. With 'yo-yo dieting' the challenge is often perceived as external such as weight-loss to please others or to achieve a certain body shape. In reality, the challenge is often internal such as low self-esteem. I once worked with a morbidly obese middle-aged lady who had been attending slimming classes off and on for years without success. In our first therapy session she described herself as 'disgusting' and 'repulsive.' By helping her to identify her self-esteem as the priority challenge, she was able to make progress towards her goal of losing weight.

Individual and collective

Distinguishing between these types of challenge can be understood in terms of responsibility. A student who decides to study for a degree is taking individual responsibility for graduating. A couple who want to improve their lifestyle are taking collective responsibility for earning more money. Where it gets harder to differentiate is when two or more people create a challenge for someone who has to take it on individually, or the other way around.

Self-imposed or imposed by others

A self-imposed challenge is when someone willingly undertakes a course of action, or deliberately creates a set of circumstances that results in a challenge for them. Whereas an imposed challenge is when someone is made to undertake a course of action, or when someone else creates a set of circumstances that results in a challenge for them.

An example of when these types of challenge can become blurred is when someone blames themselves for events that can never be down to their actions. A common example I encounter is with trauma. Tom, a former soldier in the British Army, came to see me to overcome Post-Traumatic Stress Disorder. Tom's trauma was triggered when an army friend, who took his place at the last minute on a patrol, was killed by a road-side bomb. Tom blamed himself and could not shake the belief that he should have been killed, not his friend. As a result, Tom recognised that he was maintaining the challenge his trauma represented to him.

People with low self-esteem and self-worth especially can find themselves in a perpetual state of this type of conflict. One of the characteristics of negative mindsets like these is the personalisation of imposed challenges. "I am a bad person. I deserve bad things to happen to me," is something I hear a lot. All such beliefs do is increase the amount of challenge someone faces.

Ongoing and specific

Specific challenges have a start, middle and an end, whereas ongoing challenges have no end to them or at least no end in sight. A three-year degree course is a specific challenge and caring for someone with a chronic condition is ongoing. Sometimes things are less clear cut, such as when one type turns into the other, for example, when a New Year's Resolution to lose a stone in weight by the end of March becomes an annual quest. Who we are and how we see ourselves can influence this type of challenge. Perfectionists present an ongoing challenge to themselves in their never-ending search for the perfect self, achievement or lifestyle, even if this ongoing challenge is made up of a series of specific ones.

Past, present and future

Challenges can be thought of in terms of our past, present and future. Examples of past challenges include past traumas and the impact of the circumstances in which someone grew up and the parenting styles they experienced. Types of present challenges include life changes and upheavals, such as redundancy, divorce and ill-health, and those that belong to the stage of life someone is going through. Future challenges include ones that are expected and anticipated as we move through different life phases. All three often influence the other. For example, past challenges that impact on our present and future, and future challenges that impact on our present.

Your challenges

Having looked at the nature of challenge and considered its different types, we can turn our attention to your challenges and how to overcome them. The following areas of life, in which we all want the best for ourselves, are common areas of challenge.

Use the box below to record your thoughts on these areas of challenge and what they mean to you.

Area of Challenge	Types of Challenge	Important or Unimportant
Yourself – identity, role and status		
Home and/or family life		
Relationships		
Career/professional development		
Health and wellbeing		
Financial		
Lifestyle		
Social and cultural		
Environment		

Overcoming your challenges

Having identified your challenges, their type and importance, in this section the focus will be on how you can overcome them.

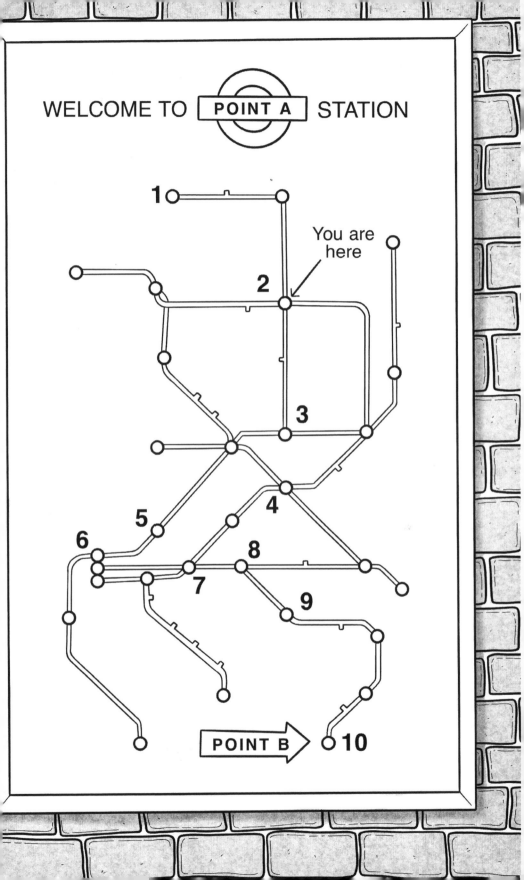

The 0-10 Challenge

Step 1 – separating your priority challenges from those that are less important. For each area of challenge and using a 0-10 scale (0 = least important, 10 = most important), choose a number that indicates how important the areas of challenge are to you. As a general rule, anything scored 7 or above can be considered a priority, 5 or 6 a lesser priority, and anything 4 or below an area that can be left possibly entirely.

Step 2 – establishing where you are and where you want to be. Taking your most important areas, choose two numbers between 0 and 10 that indicate where you are now (Point A) and where you would like to be (Point B). Reflect on the questions below:

Who:

- Who are you at Point A? For example, 'I am too unconfident.'
- Who will you be at Point B? 'I will be full of confidence.'
- Who do you need to be to get from Point A to Point B? 'I need to be brave and committed.'

What:

- What are you doing at Point A? 'I am procrastinating.'
- What will you be doing at Point B? 'I will be in a great routine.'
- What do you need to do to get from Point A to Point B? 'I need to find my entry point and put one foot in front of the other.'

The Challenge Audit

Taking each of your priority challenges, look at the 9 categories below to help you think about what you need to overcome them. Again, choose a number between 0 and 10 that represents how confident you are in each of the categories. When thinking about what you need, consider both the area and type of challenge. Any number 7 or above suggests you have enough in the categories below, 5 or 6 could be enough, but might not be, and 4 or below definitely means you have too little.

Use the box below to record your thoughts on these areas of challenge and what they mean to you.	Skills and abilities: do I have the right skills and abilities?	Confidence and self-belief: do I have enough confidence and self-belief?
Wellbeing: do I feel resilient enough?	Support: do I have the right people around me? Can they help? Will they help?	Motivation: do I feel motivated enough?
Time: am I giving myself enough time? Is this the right time?	Environment: am I in the right environment? Does it feel supportive?	Strategy: do I feel confident in my strategies? Are they helping me to make progress?

Reflecting on your numbers, consider the following questions.

1.   Resources: do I have what I need? If I don't, can

I acquire them myself or does someone else have what I need?

2.	Skills and abilities: do I have the necessary skills and abilities? If I don't, can I develop them myself or will I need support?

3.	Confidence and belief: do I have enough? If I don't, can I build these qualities on my own or will I need support?

4.	Wellbeing: do I feel resilient enough? If I don't, is my boosting my wellbeing something I can do by myself or will I need to involve someone else?

5.	Support: do I have the support I need? If I don't, who will provide it?

6.	Motivation: do I feel motivated enough? If I don't, can I motivate myself or will I need encouragement from someone else?

7.	Time: do I have enough time? If I don't, how can I find the time I need? Is this the right time? If it isn't, when will it be?

8.	Environment: am I in the right environment? Or do I need to be somewhere else?

9.	Strategy: do I have the right strategies? If I don't, how will I acquire them? By myself or with support?

"My problems started when I was unexpectedly made redundant. I was not in a good place for a long time. I listed all of my challenges and it quickly became evident that I saw every challenge as equally important. No wonder I was overwhelmed. Once I had my list of priority challenges down to a manageable number, I could see that who I was – was the problem. My whole life I thought I was an imposter, and the 0-10 challenge revealed, bluntly, who I needed to be if was to get beyond my challenges. Who I needed to be was good enough. " Sally

Summary of Chapter Five

- Challenge is a part of life and human being represent it in many ways and forms.
- We have our own relationship with challenge that can be understood in terms of our history, emotions and language.
- Making progress with our challenges means finding our 'entry point' and aligning our strategies and goals.
- Challenge can be paradoxical. It can be a challenge to turn good ideas into real ones. And there can be too little challenge, too much of it, or just the right amount (The Goldilocks Principle).
- There are many type of challenge and we need to understand our types in order to make progress.
- Overcoming our challenges involves identifying what they are and which are a priority. Once we have achieved these stages, we need to change who we are, what we do and get around the barriers we face.

T is for Transformation

Whether you move swiftly or systematically through the stages of the IMPACT model the final stage of Transformation is, of course, the stage we all wish to get to and ultimately beyond. Over the course of the previous five chapters, I have asked you to take a good look at the difficult and challenging areas of your life from the perspectives of:

1. A Conversation With IMPACT
2. Meaning
3. Patterns
4. Acceptance
5. Challenge.

In this final chapter, we will look at those areas from the perspective of transformation. As you work through this chapter, I encourage you to think of transformation as both the journey and the destination. It is the journey because in reading this book, your starting point is behind you, but your destination is still up ahead. It is the destination because you want your journey to come to an end, when who you are is who you want to be, when what you are doing is what you want to be doing, and when the life you are leading is the life you want to be leading.

When I talk of destinations, I am very aware that we might reach several as we go through life. When I talk about reaching your destination in this book, I have in mind the one you are journeying towards at this this stage of your life.

> "I thought there was a perfect destination waiting for me. All I had to do was find it. I searched and searched for my destination in each new relationship, house move, possession, job, but I was completely ignoring my journey. Learning that the journey helps to create the destination was a huge thing for me. It helped me to notice the beauty around me, and to be more appreciative of the moment. I did eventually arrive at my destination, but it was not what I expected. It was made up of everything I encountered along the way."
> Saskia

Kickstarting your transformation

> "No problem can be solved from the same level of consciousness that created it." Einstein

When someone has been trying unsuccessfully to their achieve their transformation, sometimes it is their approach to it, which has become part of the problem. Taking Einstein's quote, they are trying to find solutions from a problem-generating level of consciousness. Ever thought you were getting somewhere digging that hole? As a practitioner and an author, what I MUST achieve if I am to help someone achieve their transformation, is shift them into a solution-generating level of consciousness. How this happens is less important than what it does. A few years ago, I wrote the story below as a way of kickstarting a particular client's transformation. He was stuck and I was stuck trying to help him. The story has proven popular ever since.

Manhole cover

A man walks out of his front door and falls down an open manhole that lies right outside. To the casual observer this looks like an unfortunate accident, but what about to the man himself and his family and neighbours? No, they don't, because the thing is this man knows this circular, deep and unpleasant hazard is there. How does he know this? Because it's been there – for some time. He knows it when he wakes up, when he cleans his teeth and when he eats his breakfast. And yet each day, down he goes, into the grime and filth of the sewer below. So, far from being accidental, the man's daily fate seems somehow preordained. Is it deliberate? An act of self-punishment maybe? Who knows? Perhaps not even the man himself. What might surprise anyone reading this story, who doesn't know this man, is the number of times he has fallen down into the sewer. Actually, no one knows the exact figure other than it's a large one. And yet the solution seems so obvious. How is it that he keeps on doing something that is so demonstrably harmful? Why doesn't the penny drop? Why doesn't he just cover the hole with a manhole cover? You would, wouldn't you?

Reading my story proved to be a turning point for my client. It helped him see where and how he was going wrong in his attempts to achieve his transformation. Stories are one way—a great way—to kickstart our transformation. So are models like mine. In this chapter, I will show you a range of ideas, perspectives and approaches to help you achieve your transformation.

Transformation: who, what, where, when, why and how

As we progress on our journey what exactly are, we transforming? Or when we have reached our destination what have we transformed? For me this breaks down nicely into categories of:

- **Who**
  Clearly, we transform ourselves or aim to, but as we do, other people can also be transformed either directly or indirectly. These can be people we know or people we don't know.
- **What**
  The 'what' can refer to almost anything, but I break it down into our internal and external realities.
  The two lists overpage are not exhaustive, so if you think of your own, please add them.

Internal reality	External reality
Identity, role and status	Identity, role and status
Thoughts, behaviours and emotions	Home and family
Relationship with/perceptions of the external world	Relationships
	Academia and education
Beliefs about and perspectives	Professional
Mental and physical	Lifestyle
Past, present & future perceptions	Social and cultural
Memories	Environment
Sensory experiences	Past, present & future
Skills and abilities	Skills and abilities

- **Where**
  Transformation can happen at home, at work and in the social spaces we visit and spend time in, and it can also happen in our mental and physical selves.
- **When**
  Transformation can happen at any time of life, of course, but common examples are when it is in response to adversity; when we have embarked on a personal or professional challenge; and when we are transitioning between important life stages. Transformation can also happen in a short space of time or over longer periods.
- **Why**
  Sometimes it is because we want to and sometimes it is because we have to. The context of our lives is connected to why, such as when we are in education, forming new relationships or changing career

- **How**
  Transformation can happen by ourselves and/or with others; it can happen in a very structured and deliberate way or more haphazardly. The 'how' of transformation can be easy or hard, swift or drawn out, exciting or overwhelming.

Attention and Transformation

As human beings we have no choice but to move forwards in time and space, otherwise known as the aging process. This means we are on a journey of transformation and heading towards some kind of destination whether we like it or not. As part of this journey through life, our mind/body systems take the 'material' we give them and transform it into our reality. By material, I am referring to our daily thoughts, behaviours and emotions, plus our daily interactions and engagements with the world. Where we focus our attention is crucial in determining whether this material is, in simple terms, positive or negative.

The importance of the principles involved here for our transformation cannot be understated. Because our mind/body systems operate to some degree independently of us, it means that our transformation is partly out of our hands. Now, when the material we give our mind/body systems is positive, this is a great thing, but when it is negative, it is far from being so.

The 'trouble' with our mind/body systems is they can be very obedient. They just work with the material we give them. If it is negative, they just shrug their shoulders and get on it with it. They don't want to, but in the absence of something more positive, they are left with no choice because we have to move forwards in time and space. This is why it is so important for us to generate, and to know HOW to generate, positive material. Without it our mind/body systems cannot play their part in getting us to our desired destination along a positive journey of transformation.

Activity – what type of material are you producing?

	positive	negative
Thoughts		
Actions/Behaviours		
Feelings/Emotions		
Relationships (interaction and engagements with the outside world: people, places and objects.)		

"As a software engineer I could see immediately that I was literally programming my brain with harmful material. Thinking self-sabotaging thoughts, which had become a real issue for me, was the equivalent of programming IN a virus, not getting rid of one. Crazy. Once I understood the relationship between transformation and attention in that way, it became much easier to do something about it." Neil

A journey through time

Once you are on your journey of transformation, it will be important to know where you at any given time if you are to avoid losing your way and put arriving at your destination in doubt. Personally, I like to check how my journey of transformation is unfolding both day-by-day and across longer stretches of time. In order to know, I ask myself the following two questions:

To know day-by-day, I ask myself in the morning when I wake up:

- Is today going to be like yesterday?

To get a broader sense of where I am, I ask myself this question:

- Is my past, present and future in harmony?

Actually, there is another reason I ask myself these questions and that is because even if I don't, another part of me is. Who I hear you ask? My Emotional Self, who I have introduced to you throughout this book, that's who. My Emotional Self asks these questions as part of its ongoing monitoring and assessment of my attempts to thrive and survive. And it asks them in expectation of an answer because it wants to know if my transformation, a key part of my thriving and surviving, is on track. And because you have an Emotional Self, it means you are being asked these questions, too.

Is today going to be like yesterday?

If yesterday was a good day, then your answer needs to be, "Yes, today will be like yesterday. More of the same." If yesterday was not a good day, then your answer needs to be "No, today won't be like yesterday and this is how I will be turning things around." Our Emotional Selves love these two answers because they reassure it that you know how to keep your transformation on track through good days and bad. What your Emotional Selves don't like is either silence because you don't know the question is being asked in the first place, or answers that indicate you don't know how to repeat good days and respond to bad ones.

Is my past, present and future in harmony?

There are four important ways you can respond to this question to keep your Emotional Self happy and reassured:

- talk to them about how you will be taking into your present what has worked in your past and leaving behind what hasn't
- talk to it about how you will be maintaining and improving what is working in your present and addressing what isn't
- talk to it about how you will be taking the potential emerging in your present into your future
- talk to it about how the positive vision you have for your future will shape your present and past.

The aim is to ensure consistency across all four conversations. Inconsistency rings alarm bells for your Emotional Self. How can your present and future work out if you bring your past difficulties with you? How can your future work out if your present problems remain unresolved? Consistency reassures, excites and inspires your Emotional Self. It gives IT confidence that you are on track. To ensure consistency, you can do a spot of time-travelling. From your desired future, look back at your present to assess whether your day-to-day steps are consistent with you achieving it. Or from your present, look back at your past to make sure it is not holding you back. I read this quote once and it stuck with me: "If you want to be taken seriously be consistent." Well here is my version: "If you want to take yourself seriously be consistent."

Emotions as messages: lost or on track?

If you are feeling difficult emotions such as stress, anxiety or depression, you know your Emotional Self is not feeling reassured by how your journey is unfolding. These types of emotions are its way of communicating with you that you are lost, and you need to get your transformation back on track. If you are waking up in a good place emotionally, feeling energised and motivated, you know your Emotional Self is feeling reassured that you know where you are going. In the box below, have a go at answering the two questions.

Is today going to be like yesterday?	
Is my past, present and future in harmony?	

A helpful approach to transformation

Many people fail to achieve their transformation not because they can't, but because they have what I call an unhelpful approach to transformation. An unhelpful approach to transformation is characterised by certain problematic ways of thinking, behaving, feeling and relating. To establish whether you have an unhelpful approach or whether yours is a helpful one, have a look at the table overpage. I have listed what in my experience are common characteristics of approaches to transformation. Looking at the list, put a number between 0 and 10 next to each (0 = very unhelpful, 10 = very helpful) to establish whether you have a helpful approach to transformation, or not. A score 6 or above suggests you are making the characteristic work for you. A score of 5 suggests it is not making a difference either way. A score 4 or below suggests a characteristic that needs work.

	Score 0–10	Helpful or unhelpful?
Conversations With Impact – when you think of your existing conversations, to what degree are they helping or hindering?		
Acceptance of your current reality – how are you when things get difficult? Do you shrug your shoulders and get on with things? Stick your head in the sand? Or get angry or down?		
Commitment to doing what it takes – is adversity a good teacher for you? Do you learn from hardship and keep going or do you give up easily?		
The right level of challenge – too much challenge = easily overwhelmed. Too little = nothing gets attempted. Do you get it just right – or not?		
The right goals with the right strategies – do your goals sit on the drawing board gathering dust because you don't know what you are doing? Or do your goals leap off the drawing board because you know how to achieve them?		
Time and patience – what if something is not a quick fix? Do you settle in and see it through? Or get frustrated and give up?		
What is your self-talk like? Do you give yourself a hard time because you are a perfectionist? Or are you kind to yourself and appreciative. How positive, supportive and encouraging of to yourself are you?		
Self-belief – do you expect to fail before you have even started? Or do you back yourself?		
Viewing setbacks as opportunities – do you view setbacks and relapses as failures? Or as occurrences to learn and improve from?		

	Score 0–10	Helpful or unhelpful?
Effective ideas, knowledge and resources – when you add up all the pieces of information and knowledge, when you consider all of the resources at your disposal, are they making a difference, or not?		
The right skills and abilities – are you good at positive thinking? Are you flexible in your behaviour? Can you control your emotions? Can you get what you need from your relationships?		
The right mindset – do you think that who you are is who you will always be? Do you see things as fixed, unchangeable? Or do you think you can grow? Is the world something you can change and influence?		
'When' rather than 'If' language – are you full of doubt and uncertainty? Do you expect things not to work out? Or do you feel confident about your outcomes, pushing away your fears?		

What did you discover? Do you have an unhelpful approach to transformation, or a helpful one? When you reflect on your relationship with transformation, were you surprised by your findings or were they expected? If you have an unhelpful approach, what areas do you need to focus on to 'transform' your approach to transformation into a helpful one?

Imagined transformation is REAL transformation

When we are at the start of our transformation, not seeing any change is enough to put some people off. New Year's Resolutions are a good example of this. Once a client memorably shouted (in a nice way) at me "Transformation? What transformation?!"

In response, I asked him to take a leap of faith. "Just because you can't see it," I said, "doesn't mean it's not happening."

My client had come to see me for a crippling fear of enclosed spaces. His phobia had become so bad he was finding driving increasingly difficult and flying impossible. His approach to transformation had been unhelpful because he just couldn't get past his understandable need to see early evidence of positive transformation. Early evidence that our transformation is underway can be a morale booster, but sometimes it is not forthcoming.

What I was able to say to my client was that imagined transformation, when we rehearse it in our imagination, is known to change our brains, laying down new neural pathways. This means that at one level of consciousness our brains do not distinguish between doing something for real and doing it in our imagination. This was how I pacified my client and gave him hope. When you imagine seeing yourself comfortably in enclosed spaces, I told him, your brain accepts this. Then, when you actually place yourself in these spaces, your brain recognises what you are doing from your successful, imagined rehearsal. "You've been here before," my client's brain might have said. Through practice and repetition of both imagined and real transformation, our neural pathways are strengthened. In time they become established and our transformation is complete. In the end my client had to accept imagined transformation IS real transformation. Our final appointment came after a holiday to California, which included a drive down the famous coastal road from San Francisco to San Diego.

Too many people give up when they don't see concrete evidence of immediate change and that is a real shame.

If you are one such person, I give you my 'Ship's Rope' analogy.

The Ship's Rope

Imagine a thick piece of ship's rigging, the type found on large sailing ships. This piece of rope represents the neural pathway in your brain that contains your difficulties and challenges. The first positive step you take along your journey of transformation only frays the rope, leaving it intact and full of strength. The second step has a similar effect. For a time, steps forward leave the rope frayed, but largely complete. However, repeated fraying fatally weakens the rope, eventually snapping it. Magically, each frayed piece of rope floats towards one another and become entwined forming a new, thick piece. This new piece represents the new, strong pathway in the brain that symbolises our transformation.

Mountain Climbing

> Accepting imagined transformation is the start of our climb up the mountain prevents us falling into the trap of thinking we are always still on the ground.

One final thought on a helpful approach to transformation. Firstly, I must add that my fascination with mountain climbing is inversely related to my ability to do it. Do I get why people do it? Not really. Mountain climbing has, though, become useful to me as a practitioner. I have found it especially useful when it comes to successful transformation—reaching the summit—because of its ability to communicate a helpful approach.

- Before the climber leaves the ground, a great deal of preparation is undertaken.
- Being unable to see the summit at the start due

to cloud or bad weather does not necessarily stop someone beginning their climb or cancelling it completely.

- Once the climber has started, progress is made whether the summit is visible or not.
- The climber starts with a route in mind but accepts it might have to change along the way.
- Glimpses of the summit are allowed but the climber never really takes their eye off the bit of rock in front of them, so they don't fall.
- Risk and setbacks are accepted as occupational hazards.
- Falls are anticipated by the climber, and ropes limit how far they fall if they do.
- Ultimately the climber, if they focus patiently on the mountain in front of them, reaches the summit by putting one hand and foot in front of the other.

Stages of transformation

If we are to make our journey of transformation as smooth as possible, allowing us to arrive at our destination, knowing the stages we will go through can be important. Anticipating stages along the way, can help us to avoid too many bumps and bruises, unhelpful diversions or even being knocked off our journey completely.

Here are some stages to look out for:

Bigger visions, smaller visions

Transformation can slow, stall or reverse when the bigger vision we have for our transformation and the smaller ones that will build it are out of sync. One client of mine illustrated this problem perfectly. Anthony came to see me for severe anxiety and panic attacks. He had recently left a safe, corporate job and set up on his own creating and building bespoke furniture. Anthony and his business partner were very talented. Their customers were delighted because Anthony was able to transform their visions into a reality. Anthony had a clear vision for his business transformation, too. He saw his customers enjoying his furniture all around the world, their lifestyles transformed by his products. There was no denying this was a great vision and yet Anthony sometimes never made it to his workshop due to his anxiety and panic. Working through the IMPACT model revealed that Anthony was not attending to the mundane aspects—the smaller, day-to-day visions—for his business. Bookkeeping, material costs, time management—all were being neglected.

> "I was in denial. If you don't look, it's amazing what you won't discover. My fantasy was that business could be endless days of creating beautiful furniture. So I got myself an accountant and business advisor. It cost me money in the short-term, but it saved my business."

Cave and Continuation

My Cave or Continuation Point is the point when the new transformation we are committed to achieving comes into conflict with the life it is intended to replace. It is when we realise, sometimes cruelly, that the transformation we are after will not be achieved by a single burst of effort; when we discover that our transformation will be made up of a series of hard fought, hard won smaller transformations. The New Year's Resolution is a perfect example of a journey of transformation beset by regular Cave and Continuation Points. Whether we cave and fall back into our previous way of living, or whether we continue into our desired new one, will depend on how we think, behave, feel, and form our relationships at our Cave and Continuation Points. The MOST important factor is whether continuing is MORE emotionally persuasive than caving. If it isn't, then we will cave. Whether it is losing weight, changing jobs or improving our mental health, succeeding on our journey of transformation requires us to put in place the right strategies to ensure we get through this stage.

Divorcing the action from the feeling

As I have suggested, one of the most frustrating things about transformation can be the lack of emotional reward for our best efforts. My idea 'divorcing the action from the feeling' offers an explanation for this lack of 'reward.' When we are seeking to transform our difficulties and challenges, new actions still come, frustratingly, with old feelings. This is because our Emotional Selves lag behind us. Why it does might surprise you; they are protecting us. Our Emotional Selves understand what is required for successful transformation. They also understand the pain of failing, so to protect us they keep us in our original emotional state until we present them with sustained evidence our transformation will happen. When it has enough evidence, it catches up with us and gives us our emotional reward.

Divorcing the action from the feeling happens in four stages:

- Stage one is when our Emotional Self observes our new actions, appreciates that some form of change is clearly underway, but waits to see what unfolds.
- Stage two is when our Emotional Self is open to the idea of disconnecting old emotions from our new actions as we present it with more evidence.
- Stage three is when we have presented enough evidence to persuade our Emotional Self to divorce old feelings from our new actions. For a time, our new actions exist in an emotional limbo, attached to neither old nor new emotions.
- Stage four is when our Emotional Self, realising the need to take us out of our emotional limbo, connects new emotions to our now established actions.

Purposeful drifting

I developed my 'purposeful drifting' idea during my career in higher education as a student coach and therapist. In my work, I came across two types of student. One who knew what they wanted to do after graduating, one who did not. The students who lacked a clear vision for life after university were often understandably anxious, and I always wanted to give them a positive perspective on the life ahead of them. To these students, I suggested purposeful drifting. This idea was born out of my own experiences after leaving university. Although I spectacularly failed to appreciate this at the time, my own transformation into who I am now and what I have become were born in those days. Looking back, I thought I was drifting aimlessly, but now I know better. For good and sometimes for bad, I gathered and learnt so much about myself and life in that time. Knowing I was purposefully drifting meant I would have appreciated this. If your vision of transformation is proving elusive, know that the experiences you are gathering along your journey contain coordinates for your destination. So, allow yourself a period of purposeful drifting if your destination is unclear.

Putting your transformation together

I have designed the IMPACT model to help you whether you know exactly what areas of your life to transform, or whether you are still working things out. If you have a good idea of the areas you wish to transform, the next activity is to list them in order of priority. Overpage is a list of the areas that have featured throughout this book. Using a 0-10 scale put a number next to each area where 0 = an area is completely unimportant and 10 = very important. My suggestion is that any area you score 6 or above, are your priority areas, and any scored 5 or below can be either put to one side or dismissed entirely.

If you are still working things out, you can still use the 0-10 scale, but this time use the scale to measure degrees of certainty. Put a 0 if you are fairly sure an area isn't a priority and a 10 if you think an area probably is.

Areas of transformation:

Your internal reality

- Identity, role and status.
- Thoughts, behaviours and emotions.
- Our internal relationship with the external world.
- Beliefs about and perspectives on life.
- Mental and physical health.
- Past, present & future

  - Memories
  - Immediate experiences
  - Future visions.

Your external reality

- Identity, role and status.
- Home and family life.
- Relationships.
- Academia and education.
- Professional life.
- Lifestyle.
- Social and cultural life.
- Environment.
- Past, present & future.

What did you discover? Do your chosen areas—or possible areas—make sense to you as you look back over this and the previous five stages of the IMPACT model? Over the next few pages, are some exercises that can help you go further on your journey and closer towards your destination.

Rewriting your story

Imagine you and I are sat in a theatre. We are part of the audience, but we are also the director, producer and scriptwriter. Sat high up, we have a good view of the stage and the play being acted out. The play is very familiar because it is your life being told. From time to time we look around and notice the audience dwindling in size. More and more of the audience continue to leave. You decide to catch someone and ask them why they are leaving. You are told the play no longer grabs their imagination. It's the same story night after night. Someone walking past says it's like the film Groundhog Day. You and I look at one another and realise that we are now the only people left. We agree something needs to change and call down to the actors asking them to stop. As the producer, director and scriptwriter, we knock our creative heads together. Your story has lost the power to bring in an audience, so the story needs to change. A week later we hand out a new script to the actors, who respond with energy and enthusiasm. A week later the opening night is a great success and the final curtain is met with rapturous applause. You grab a departing audience member and ask them what they loved about the play. "The main character, they transformed themselves. There was no hope in the old play," they say, "whereas this one was full of it." Another audience member leans over their seat and talks about the pivotal scene, the one when we all cheered and shouted. You express your gratitude and sit back while the theatre empties of an inspired audience.

The 'brain as theatre' has proven to be a helpful metaphor in my work. The brain is the building, the play, props, actors and crew. However, when overcoming our difficulties and challenges proves impossible, it can feel like we have lost control of our own play. It can feel like the theatre itself is deciding which play to put on. My IMPACT model puts you as the producer, director and scriptwriter back in charge. It puts you back in control of your own story.

Activity

Your story so far	The plot twist: your story from now on

Darwinian Tree

Sometimes it can be hard to generate ideas that make progress on our journey possible and reaching our destination a reality. My Darwinian Tree exercise (page 151) can resolve this creative and imaginative struggle by allowing any emerging, abstract ideas to 'evolve' into concrete ones that can be acted upon. In my experience, great ideas are often just below the surface in our unconscious, but to shift them into our conscious awareness, requires some coaxing.

- Step one: in the middle write down the difficulty or challenge you want to resolve.
- Step two: spend a brief amount of time—no more than 10 minutes—record any emerging ideas that offer a possible resolution to your difficulty or challenge. Note them down at the end of the first circle of 'evolutionary' branches. It is vital that you write down whatever emerges. You must trust your Unconscious Self to offer you something useful. Don't question or dismiss at this stage. If you spend more than 10 minutes on your initial ideas, it can become too easy to make the struggle worse.
- Step three: come back to your Darwinian Tree a day or so later. At the end of the second circle of evolutionary branches, note down any new ideas that emerge from the first. Again, limit your time to 10 minutes or less.
- Step four: repeat.
- Step five: repeat until your ideas have become ones you can act on.

The chances are that as you progress outwards, some of your

initial ideas will fall away. That is ok because those that don't will be ones with real potential and obvious ways to take them further.

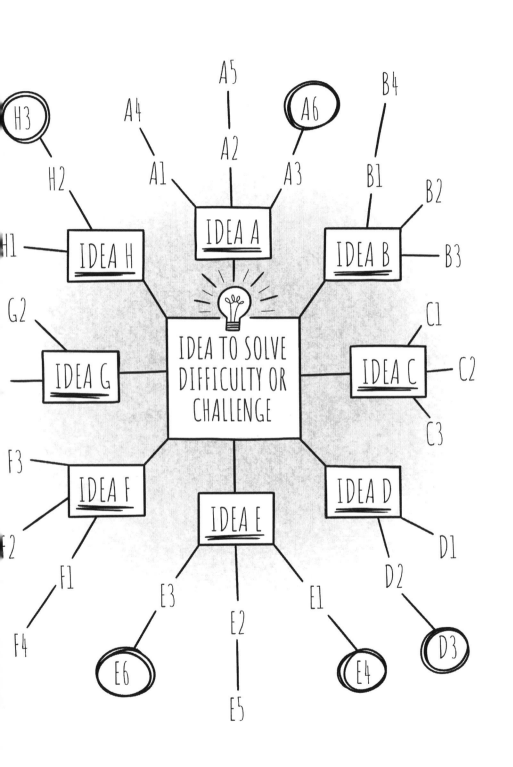

STEP ONE

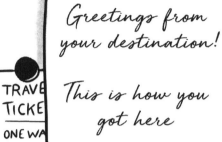

Greetings from your destination!

This is how you got here

TRAVE
TICKE
ONE WA

STEP TWO

Projections

STEP THREE

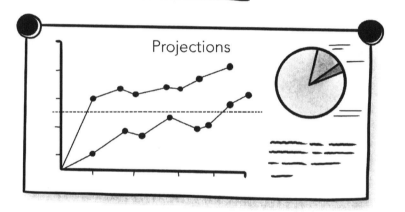

September

GOAL!

The Destination Finder

"To know the road ahead, ask those coming back."
Chinese proverb

My Destination Finder activity starts at the end of your journey when you have reached your destination. It may seem odd to start at the end of the journey, but throughout this chapter (and book) I have used our ability to 'time-travel' through our past, present and future. There are three reasons for this:

- In 'Attention and Transformation' I said that our brains actively bring about what we focus our attention on. Imagining our destination can be seen as an instruction to our brains to get to work on making it a reality.
- In 'Imagined transformation is real transformation' I said that when we imagine something, at one level our brains accept it is real, and as a result lays down neural pathways that contain what we imagine, in this case our destination.
- If our destination has been reached, it means we must have completed our journey. Therefore, we can state what steps we must have completed at stages along our journey.

Step One: establish your current reality: what is happening now?

Step Two: establish your desired future: how would you like things to be at your destination?

Step Three: establish a timeline of when this transformation might occur e.g. a month, 6 months or a year.

Step Four: take some time to deepen the 'vision' of your destination. Make it a multisensory experience: imagine, engage and fully 'embody' this future state for yourself. Some questions you can ask are:

- What is happening?
- What do you see?
- How do you feel?
- What has changed?
- How have you changed?

Speak to yourself as if your desired future were a reality i.e. use the present tense such as 'I am doing this, I am doing that...'

Step Five: from this future state look back and describe how you got there, identifying the milestones you reached along the way. Starting at your destination, travel back to the penultimate stage, then the stage before that and so on. At each stage speak from the present, as if your objective has been achieved e.g. "I did this to get to this stage," or "I did that to move to the next stage."

Step Six: Then bring yourself back to the present—the now—and explore what this exercise has given you in terms of learning, understanding and insight. Confirm your next actions based on the exercise.

Step Seven: approach this exercise as a work in progress. Repeat it on a regular basis to ensure that you are still working effectively towards your destination and identifying any issues that need resolving. My suggestion is to do Destination Finder weekly, but you can experiment to find out what works for you.

And finally: stories of transformation

I use a lot of short stories in my work because if stories are about anything, it is transformation. So, I hope you enjoy the stories over the next few pages and that along with my IMPACT Model, they inspire you to achieve the transformation you are after.

Fast-flowing river

Imagine you are being swept along by a fast-flowing river. Try as you might, the current is too strong for you to swim to the riverbanks. Terrified and weak, you are at the mercy of the raging waters. Suddenly up ahead you notice a fallen tree that has been felled by a lightning strike, maybe from the storm that caused your river to flood. A branch from the tree reaches out across the river.

You feel and hear a loud smack as your hands connect with and grip the branch. The water still pushes against your waist and legs, but your new situation quickly sinks in - you are still in the fast-flowing river but no longer being swept along by it. As your mind clears, two options present themselves. Drop back down into the river? Shimmy along the branch?

With a thud, you land on the riverbank, your knees bending to cushion your landing. Still in a state of shock and disbelief, you look down for reassurance. Yes, there are your two feet, a bit battered and bruised but definitely connected to solid ground. For a few moments, you enjoy feeling connected to the riverbank before asking what next? Jump back into the river? There is a definite pull. After all, you were in it for a long time. Or climb to the top of the riverbank?

At the top of the riverbank, you look down over the other

side. Several paths lead away into the distance. All paths look interesting to you but one in particular draws your attention. Checking in with your gut instinct, you choose the path directly ahead of you. You feel the movement of your body as it finds a nice rhythm. The noise of the river still penetrates your senses, but it dims with each step. And then you don't hear it at all.

The young man and the Buddha

A long time ago in the East lived a young man who, after suffering a run of bad luck, had slipped into such a state of despair that life didn't seem worth living. One night while drowning his sorrows in a bar he overheard one customer telling a story to another about how the Buddha can work miracles for people and help them put their lives back together. Intrigued and prepared to give it one last shot he set off to see the Buddha the very next morning.

On arrival at the Buddha's great palace he begged an audience with him. The Buddha was happy to see the young man, who proceeded to tell him of the story he had heard and whether it was true – could he perform miracles and help him put his life back together? The Buddha confirmed the details of the story and said that he could indeed help him. However, before they could get started the young man must undertake some simple tasks that the Buddha was too busy to do himself. After the tasks were completed then the miracles would begin.

The tasks involved visiting the homes of three people who lived nearby and who, incidentally, had also experienced misfortune in life. He was to bring back something from each of them. "What shall I bring back?" The young man asked.

"Oh, anything useful," replied the Buddha.

A little perplexed the young man set off. The first person to be visited was a local farmer who the young man found working hard in a corn field. The farmer asked the young man why he had come. His visitor explained the whole story from start to finish, about his misfortune, his meeting with the Buddha and the need to return with a useful object. The farmer thought for a few moments and said, "I will give your something far more useful than a simple object—I will give you knowledge." And so he took his troubled visitor and taught him how to sow, grow and harvest a field of corn until this knowledge was firmly planted in the young man's mind. Still a little confused the young man nevertheless thanked the farmer. As he was about to leave, he remarked to the farmer that he did not appear to be suffering any misfortune now. The farmer simply smiled and said he too had been to see the Buddha.

The next rendezvous was with an axe maker who, having enquired as to the reason for the young man's visit, was regaled with the same story told to the farmer. The axe maker smiled knowingly, cast his gaze around his workshop and seeing one of his finest axes picked it up and handed it to the young man. And then the young man did something he never would have thought possible only a week ago – he asked the axe maker how to make axes. "Show me how to do it so I can do it for myself," he asked.

Having acquired his second new skill it was time for him to leave. "And what of your misfortune the Buddha spoke about?" he asked the axe maker.

"Oh that," reflected the craftsman, "that disappeared shortly after my trip to see the Buddha. Who do you need to see next by the way?"

The young man replied that he must visit the saddle maker. "Does he live near here?"

"Not far," came the reply, "you're much closer than you might think." And so he set off to find the saddle maker and when he found him he discovered a similar story to those of the farmer and the axe maker. He left, of course, with a brand new saddle to add to his corn and axe—a saddle he had made himself.

At his second audience with the Buddha the young man felt a little more positive. He couldn't help feeling motivated by the three people he had just visited and the new knowledge and skills he had gained. If they can overcome their misfortune so can I, he reflected. Indeed the Buddha commented on the obvious change in the young man's appearance – for the better. His young student agreed that he was indeed feeling more positive and explained that he had found his tasks very rewarding.

But this newfound optimism was dented when the Buddha announced that the miracles would have to wait a while longer as he must undertake an important journey. The young man could not hide his disappointment and he felt that old feeling of despair start to return, but just as he felt it start to overwhelm him his attention was distracted by a loud exclamation from the Buddha. "Ah!" said his illustrious teacher. "Now it is I who need your help."

"But how can I help you, of all people?" worried the young man.

The Buddha explained that he was ill-prepared for his trip and needed certain supplies to make it possible: some corn to make bread, an axe to chop wood for his fire and a good saddle for his horse. I have none of these things, exclaimed the Buddha, and I can't make any of them either. The young man suddenly felt a profound sense of calmness descend on him as he realised for the first time in a long time that he had something to offer. In that instant he realised too that this calmness was his reward for having confronted and dealt with his difficulties. He proudly informed the Buddha that yes he could be of help to him. The young man then threw himself enthusiastically into his tasks and in no time at all he was waving farewell to his wise mentor as he embarked on his journey.

It was some months before the Buddha returned to make good his side of the bargain and relieve the young man of his misery by miracle. On his return the Buddha thanked him for the corn, sturdy axe and comfortable saddle for without these things his trip would have been a disaster. Having then shown an interest in the Buddha's trip the young man fell silent for a while as if lost in his thoughts. The Buddha, seeing this distant look, decided that now was the time to perform his miracle and he began making preparations to do so. These preparations shook the young man out of his peaceful trance. He stepped forward and gently taking hold of the Buddha's arm told him not to bother as the miracles had already been performed.

Moving On

In an ancient land there was once a market stall holder who plied his trade along a busy road joining two thriving cities. Each day he counted his blessings for having found such a lucrative site because the whole world, it seemed, travelled up and down that road as they went about whatever was their

159

business. In the middle of their journeys the travellers got thirsty and hungry, craving rest and refreshment, needs that our market stall holder was more than happy to provide for. As the money rolled in and he became wealthy, so he became determined, more than determined even, to stay rooted to that spot. Nothing and nobody he promised himself would persuade him to let go of his pitch and move on.

But as is the way of the world times changed. New towns and cities grew up across the land drawing people and traffic away from the road. And as is another way of the world there are those who understand the inevitability of change and the need to go with it and those who don't. And our market stall holder was one of those who didn't want to…let go and move on. "Why should I?" he would say defensively to his dwindling band of customers. Business will pick up, he convinced himself, and having fought and worked so hard, having enjoyed the fruits of his labour, he had too much personal investment in staying put. He developed business strategies aimed at attracting people back to the area. He invested more of his money and of himself, becoming ever more determined to stay put even as those around him were packing up.

One particular day, a bad day in fact for our market stall holder as business was especially poor, a man approached on a horse and dismounted in front of the stall. His horse was a fine one, our trader noted, as were his clothes which were clearly made of the finest cloth. But aside from his finery something else caught the eye of our trader: it was the man's look – untroubled, tranquil, at peace with the world.

Peering into the stall the stranger saw a dejected figure and glancing around he saw precious few reasons for this miserable tradesman to be here. Engaging him in conversation the stranger asked how he had arrived at this particular spot. In reply and touched that someone was taking an interest in him, our trader recounted how he had spotted the opportunity to set up and start trading. He had foreseen that the road would attract more and more people because the two cities it connected were growing. His previous business wasn't going anywhere, he continued, and letting that go and moving on seemed the natural thing to do. Much to his surprise the hero of our story repeated these words quietly to himself— "the natural thing to do." Both men sensed the meaning of the moment. A few seconds of silence passed between them, but in our hero's mind were born the first stirrings of potential, of possibility.

Dropping some pennies into the trader's hands, the nameless rider thanked him for the food and drink he had bought and rode on. The market stall holder combined them with his meagre takings from the day. He loosened the ropes that bound his stall tightly to poles which he in-turn loosened and lifted out of the ground.

Had anyone noticed him as he closed down for the day, they would have seen him go about his business more freely. And had anyone asked him what was going on inside his head he would have told them that, like the magnificent birds of prey circling high above on warm currents of air, the words 'letting go and moving on' were also circling magnificently on the warm currents of his imagination.

As the sun rose the next day, no market stall could be seen.

Summary of Chapter Six

- Transformation is both the journey and the destination.
- Transformation can be understood in terms of who, what, where, when, why and how.
- There is a close relationship between where we focus our attention and how our transformation unfolds.
- Transformation involves us travelling through time and visiting our past, present and future.
- There are helpful and unhelpful approaches to transformation.
- Imagined transformation is real transformation.
- There are different stages of transformation.
- Transformation can be achieved in many ways such as storytelling, patiently evolving ideas and using our desired destination to show us the journey we need to take.
- Stories are a great source of inspiration.

A Final Thought

As you reach the end of The IMPACT Model – as we finish the conversation with impact we have had together throughout my book – this could be the start of how you will transform your life with IMPACT. While you might already be well on your way to overcoming your difficulties and achieving your challenges, please keep coming back to the book, the model and its six stages. Like a good story, it has the potential to give you something new each time, enabling you: to leave with more than you came in with.

So, as you contemplate your difficulties and challenges, remember to:

- change your conversations into conversations with IMPACT.
- find MEANING and make sense of why things are as they are.
- take a step back from your PATTERNS, identify those that are helping and those that are not.
- be brave and find ACCEPTANCE in who you are, what you are doing and the life you are leading.
- make CHALLENGE work for you, not against you. Remember The Goldilocks Principle: not too little challenge, not too much, but just right.
- learn the art of TRANSFORMATION so you can enjoy both the journey and arrive at your destination.

www.conversationswithimpact.co.uk

About the Author

Mark Evans has been a coach and therapist since 2005. He has worked in Higher Education, the Employee Assistance Industry and since 2015 has run his own business Conversations With Impact. Mark is a qualified Human Givens Therapist and a European Mentoring & Coaching Council Accredited Coach Practitioner. Prior to his career in coaching and therapy, Mark worked for MIND as a Mental Health Advocate and in media advertising for The Telegraph Group.

Mark has a passion for supporting people to turn their lives around, a passion that comes from knowing that what he does can be both life-changing and sometimes life-saving.

He enjoys a pint of real ale, walking in The Peak District and eating Indian food as often as possible.

Contact info

Website: www.conversationswithimpact.co.uk

Email: info@conversationswithimpact.co.uk

Printed in Great Britain
by Amazon